Ivan Kushnir

Economy of Congo

Series "Economy in countries"

first published: 2019
last updated: 2021-01-26

Ivan Kushnir. Economy of Congo. Series "Economy in countries". - 2019. - 71 pages.

This book about the economy of Congo from the 1970s to the 2010s. Source data from UN Data.

Size. In the 2010s, the GDP of Congo was equal to $14.2 billion per year; the value of agriculture was $747.2 million; the value of industry was $6.4 billion. Since the share in the world is between .01% and .1%, the country is classified as a small economy.

Productivity. In the 2010s, the GDP per capita was $2 955.8, the value of agriculture per capita was $155.3, the value of industry per capita was $1 333.4. Since the productivity is less the average below average, the economy is classified as least developed.

Growth. In the 2010s, the growth of gross domestic product was 0.011%; the growth of agriculture was 3.8%; the growth of industry was 1.7%.

Structure. In the 2010s, the economy of Congo included: industry (47.4%), services (18.9%), trade (11.0%), construction (10.3%), transportation (7.0%), and agriculture (5.5%).

Exports and imports. In the 2010s, the exports were 11.6% higher than the imports, the net exports were equal to 6.2% of the GDP. The technological structure of exports are not better than the structure of imports.

Consumption and reproduction. The attitude of reproduction to the consumption is better than the global average, so the share of GDP in the world will increase.

Series "Economy in countries": parallel.page.link/en

ISBN: 9781795012041

Contents

Part I. Size

	The 2010s
GDP	$14.2 billion
The share in the world	0.018%
Share in Africa	0.61%
Share in Middle Africa	5.9%

Chapter I. Gross domestic product

The GDP of Congo rose from $666.1 million per year in the 1970s to $14.2 billion per year in the 2010s, that is by $13.6 billion or 21.3 times. The change occurred at $11.3 billion due to a 4.9-fold increase in prices, as also at $821.1 million due to a 1.4-fold increase in productivity, as well as at $1.4 billion due to the growing in population. The average annual growth in gross domestic product is 3.3%. The minimum value of gross domestic product was in 1970 at $283.7 million. The maximum value of GDP was in 2013 at $18.0 billion.

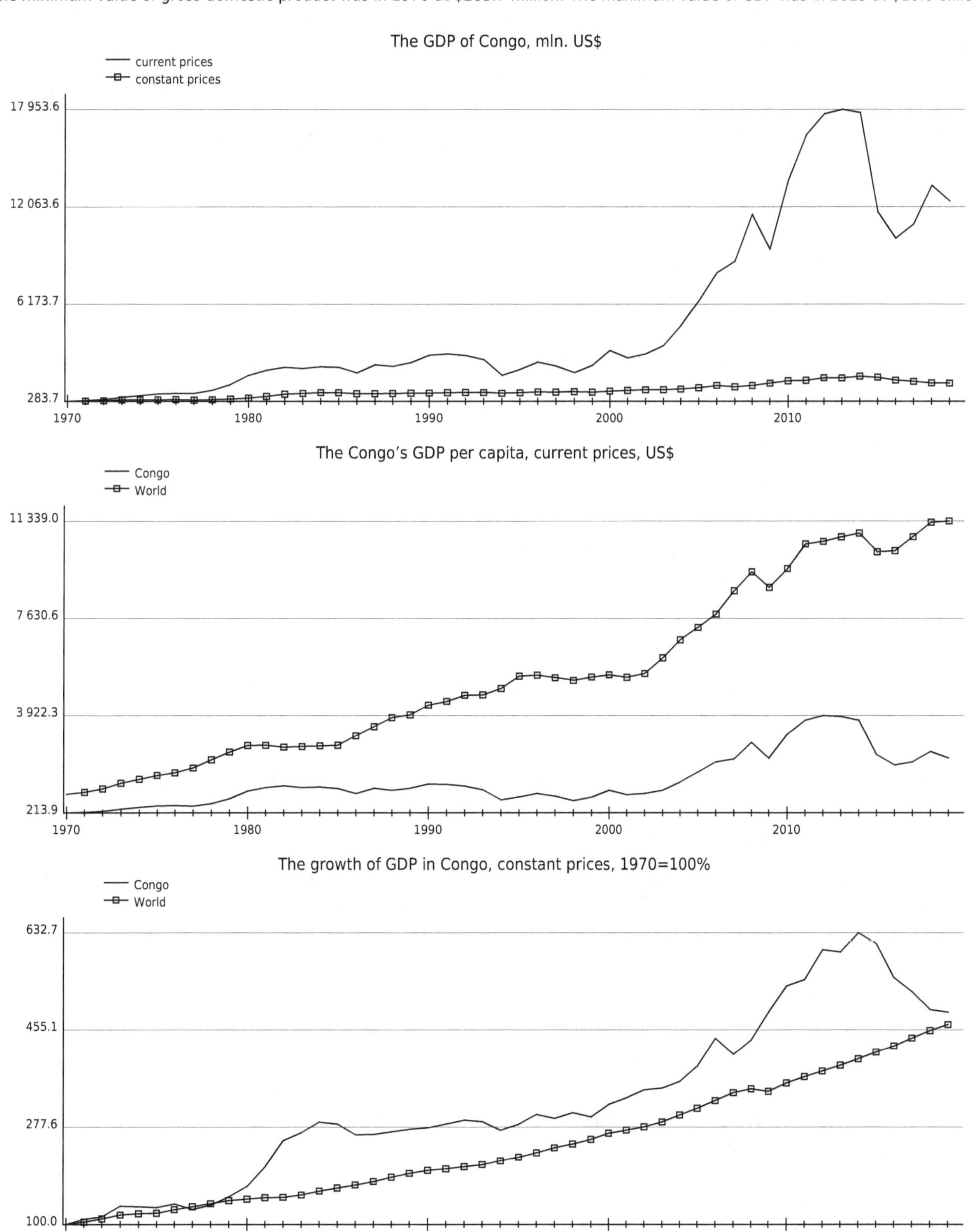

The 1970s

The gross domestic product of Congo was $666.1 million per year in the 1970s, ranked 123rd in the world, and was on a par with French Polynesia ($678.9 million). The share in the world was 0.010%, and 0.25% in Africa.

The gross domestic product of Congo consisted of: household consumption expenditure (81.6%), capital formation (48.2%), and government expenditure (22.7%).

The GDP per capita in Congo was $438.4 in the 1970s, ranked 133rd in the world, and was on a par with the Maldives ($435.8), Tonga ($430.2). The gross domestic product per capita in Congo was less than gross domestic product per capita in the world ($1 620.8) in 3.7 times, and was less than GDP per capita in Africa ($648.3) by 32.4%.

The growth of gross domestic product in Congo was 4.6% in the 1970s, ranked 86th in the world, and was on a par with the Caribbean (4.6%), Puerto Rico (4.6%), Japan (4.6%). The growth of gross domestic product in Congo (4.6%) was greater than growth of GDP in the world (4.1%), was greater than growth of gross domestic product in Africa (4.5%).

Comparison with neighbors. The GDP of Congo was greater than in the CAR ($557.7 million); but less than in DR Congo ($9.6 billion), in Angola ($4.5 billion), in Cameroon ($3.6 billion), and in Gabon ($2.1 billion). The GDP per capita in Congo was greater than in DR Congo ($424.9) and in the CAR ($285.2); but less than in Gabon ($3.3 thousand), in Angola ($654.8), and in Cameroon ($492.8). The growth of gross domestic product in Congo was greater than in the CAR (1.00%), in Angola (0.23%), and in DR Congo (0.22%); but less than in Gabon (8.2%) and in Cameroon (5.8%).

Comparison with leaders. The Congo's GDP was less than in the United States ($1.7 trillion), in the USSR ($649.4 billion), in Japan ($558.0 billion), in Germany ($484.2 billion), and in France ($333.2 billion). The Congo's GDP per capita was less than in the USA ($7.8 thousand), in France ($6.2 thousand), in Germany ($6.1 thousand), in Japan ($5.0 thousand), and in the USSR ($2.6 thousand). The growth of GDP in Congo was greater than in France (3.9%), in the United States (3.5%), and in Germany (3.1%); but less than in the USSR (4.8%) and in Japan (4.6%).

The 1980s

The Congo's GDP was $2.3 billion per year in the 1980s, ranked 114th in the world, and was on a par with Malawi ($2.3 billion), Polynesia ($2.3 billion). The share in the world was 0.015%, and 0.42% in Africa.

The gross domestic product of Congo included: household expenditure (67.9%), capital formation (55.3%), and public expenditure (18.3%).

The gross domestic product per capita in Congo was $1 124.9 in the 1980s, ranked 112th in the world, and was on a par with Northern Africa ($1 136.5), Zimbabwe ($1 142.3). The GDP per capita in Congo was less than GDP per capita in the world ($3 123.4) in 2.8 times, and was greater than gross domestic product per capita in Africa ($993.3) by 13.2%.

The growth of gross domestic product in Congo was 6.2% in the 1980s, ranked 22nd in the world, and was on a par with Mongolia (6.3%). The growth of gross domestic product in Congo (6.2%) was greater than growth of gross domestic product in the world (3.0%), was greater than growth of GDP in Africa (1.8%).

Comparison with neighbors. The GDP of Congo was greater than in the Central African Republic ($1.1 billion); but less than in DR Congo ($10.8 billion), in Cameroon ($10.7 billion), in Angola ($8.5 billion), and in Gabon ($4.6 billion). The GDP per capita in Congo was greater than in Cameroon ($1 073.3), in Angola ($868.9), in the Central African Republic ($433.9), and in DR Congo ($365.6); but less than in Gabon ($5.6 thousand). The growth of GDP in Congo was greater than in Angola (2.7%), in Cameroon (2.6%), in DR Congo (1.8%), in Gabon (1.5%), and in the Central African Republic (0.57%).

Comparison with leaders. The Congo's gross domestic product was less than in the USA ($4.2 trillion), in Japan ($1.8 trillion), in Germany ($990.0 billion), in the USSR ($887.0 billion), and in France ($729.5 billion). The GDP per capita in Congo was less than in the USA ($17.4 thousand), in Japan ($15.0 thousand), in France ($12.9 thousand), in Germany ($12.7 thousand), and in the USSR ($3.2 thousand). The growth of GDP in Congo was greater than in the USSR (4.3%), in Japan (4.3%), in the United States (3.1%), in France (2.3%), and in Germany (1.9%).

The 1990s

The Congo's gross domestic product was $2.6 billion per year in the 1990s, ranked 144th in the world, and was on a par with Bermuda

($2.6 billion). The share in the world was 0.0090%, and 0.44% in Africa.

The gross domestic product of Congo included: household expenditure (60.4%), government expenditure (28.0%), and capital formation (27.3%).

The Congo's GDP per capita was $957.8 in the 1990s, ranked 140th in the world, and was on a par with Indonesia ($953.4). The GDP per capita in Congo was less than gross domestic product per capita in the world ($5 020.1) in 5.2 times, and was greater than gross domestic product per capita in Africa ($833.3) by 14.9%.

The growth of GDP in Congo was 0.8% in the 1990s, ranked 165th in the world, and was on a par with Slovakia (0.79%). The growth of gross domestic product in Congo (0.79%) was less than growth of GDP in the world (2.8%), was less than growth of GDP in Africa (2.4%).

Comparison with neighbors. The Congo's gross domestic product was greater than in the CAR ($1.2 billion); but less than in Angola ($11.8 billion), in DR Congo ($11.4 billion), in Cameroon ($11.0 billion), and in Gabon ($5.7 billion). The GDP per capita in Congo was greater than in Angola ($857.9), in Cameroon ($818.9), in the Central African Republic ($374.8), and in DR Congo ($281.8); but less than in Gabon ($5.3 thousand). The growth of gross domestic product in Congo was greater than in Cameroon (0.70%) and in DR Congo (-5.6%); but less than in Gabon (2.1%), in the CAR (1.6%), and in Angola (0.89%).

Comparison with leaders. The Congo's gross domestic product was less than in the United States ($7.6 trillion), in Japan ($4.3 trillion), in Germany ($2.2 trillion), in France ($1.4 trillion), and in the UK ($1.3 trillion). The Congo's gross domestic product per capita was less than in Japan ($34.3 thousand), in the United States ($28.7 thousand), in Germany ($27.0 thousand), in France ($24.1 thousand), and in the United Kingdom ($22.9 thousand). The growth of gross domestic product in Congo was less than in the United States (3.2%), in the UK (2.3%), in Germany (2.2%), in France (2.0%), and in Japan (1.5%).

The 2000s

The gross domestic product of Congo was $6.2 billion per year in the 2000s, ranked 134th in the world, and was on a par with Polynesia ($6.3 billion), Malta ($6.3 billion), Mali ($6.2 billion). The share in the world was 0.013%, and 0.56% in Africa.

The gross domestic product of Congo consisted of: capital formation (37.2%), household consumption expenditure (36.3%), government expenditure (15.1%), and net export (12.4%).

The Congo's GDP per capita was $1 729.3 in the 2000s, ranked 141st in the world, and was on a par with Syria ($1 712.8), Central Asia ($1 757.0). The gross domestic product per capita in Congo was less than GDP per capita in the world ($7 176.3) in 4.1 times, and was greater than gross domestic product per capita in Africa ($1 228.8) by 40.7%.

The growth of gross domestic product in Congo was 5.1% in the 2000s, ranked 54th in the world, and was on a par with Lebanon (5.1%), South-Eastern Asia (5.1%), Indonesia (5.1%). The growth of GDP in Congo (5.1%) was greater than growth of gross domestic product in the world (3.0%), was less than growth of GDP in Africa (5.1%).

Comparison with neighbors. The gross domestic product of Congo was greater than in the CAR ($1.4 billion); but less than in Angola ($39.4 billion), in Cameroon ($17.6 billion), in DR Congo ($12.6 billion), and in Gabon ($9.1 billion). The Congo's gross domestic product per capita was greater than in Cameroon ($1 002.9), in the CAR ($357.3), and in DR Congo ($232.5); but less than in Gabon ($6.5 thousand) and in Angola ($2.0 thousand). The growth of gross domestic product in Congo was greater than in Cameroon (3.9%), in DR Congo (3.2%), in the Central African Republic (1.4%), and in Gabon (0.29%); but less than in Angola (8.6%).

Comparison with leaders. The Congo's GDP was less than in the USA ($12.6 trillion), in Japan ($4.7 trillion), in Germany ($2.8 trillion), in China ($2.6 trillion), and in the UK ($2.3 trillion). The GDP per capita in Congo was less than in the United States ($42.8 thousand), in the UK ($38.4 thousand), in Japan ($36.4 thousand), in Germany ($34.0 thousand), and in China ($1 954.1). The growth of GDP in Congo was greater than in the United States (1.9%), in the UK (1.7%), in Germany (0.73%), and in Japan (0.50%); but less than in China (10.3%).

The 2010s

The GDP of Congo was $14.2 billion per year in the 2010s, ranked 126th in the world, and was on a par with Mali ($14.1 billion), Palestine ($13.9 billion), Jamaica ($14.5 billion). The share in the world was 0.018%, and 0.61% in Africa.

The gross domestic product of Congo included: capital formation (46.5%), household consumption expenditure (31.7%), government expenditure (15.6%), and net export (6.2%).

The gross domestic product per capita in Congo was $2 955.8 in the 2010s, ranked 147th in the world, and was on a par with Bolivia ($3.0 thousand), Egypt ($2.9 thousand). The GDP per capita in Congo was less than gross domestic product per capita in the world ($10 603.1) in 3.6 times, and was greater than gross domestic product per capita in Africa ($1 979.5) by 49.3%.

The growth of GDP in Congo was 0% in the 2010s, ranked 194th in the world. The growth of GDP in Congo (0.011%) was less than growth of GDP in the world (3.1%), was less than growth of GDP in Africa (2.9%).

Comparison with neighbors. The GDP of Congo was 6.9 times higher than in the CAR ($2.1 billion); but 8.0 times lower than in Angola ($113.2 billion), 2.5 times lower than in DR Congo ($35.6 billion), 2.3 times lower than in Cameroon ($32.8 billion), and 12.6% lower than in Gabon ($16.3 billion). The Congo's GDP per capita was 2.1 times higher than in Cameroon ($1 423.9), 6.3 times higher than in DR Congo ($472.5), and 6.5 times higher than in the CAR ($458.0); but 2.9 times lower than in Gabon ($8.5 thousand) and 28.2% lower than in Angola ($4.1 thousand). The growth of GDP in Congo was greater than in the Central African Republic (-1.2%); but less than in DR Congo (6.2%), in Cameroon (4.5%), in Gabon (4.1%), and in Angola (2.1%).

Comparison with leaders. The Congo's GDP was 1 263.1 times lower than in the USA ($18.0 trillion), 738.8 times lower than in China ($10.5 trillion), 367.7 times lower than in Japan ($5.2 trillion), 257.5 times lower than in Germany ($3.7 trillion), and 194.6 times lower than in the United Kingdom ($2.8 trillion). The Congo's GDP per capita was 19.0 times lower than in the USA ($56.2 thousand), 15.1 times lower than in Germany ($44.7 thousand), 14.3 times lower than in the United Kingdom ($42.2 thousand), 13.8 times lower than in Japan ($40.9 thousand), and 2.5 times lower than in China ($7.5 thousand). The growth of gross domestic product in Congo was less than in China (7.7%), in the United States (2.3%), in Germany (1.9%), in the United Kingdom (1.8%), and in Japan (1.3%).

Chapter II. Value added

The value added of Congo increased from $829.0 million per year in the 1970s to $13.5 billion per year in the 2010s, that is by $12.7 billion or 16.3 times. The change occurred at $9.2 billion due to a 3.1-fold increase in prices, as also at $1.7 billion due to a 1.6-fold increase in productivity, as well as at $1.8 billion due to the growth in population. The average annual growth in value added is 4.1%. The minimum value of value added was in 1970 at $362.1 million. The maximum value of value added was in 2013 at $17.1 billion.

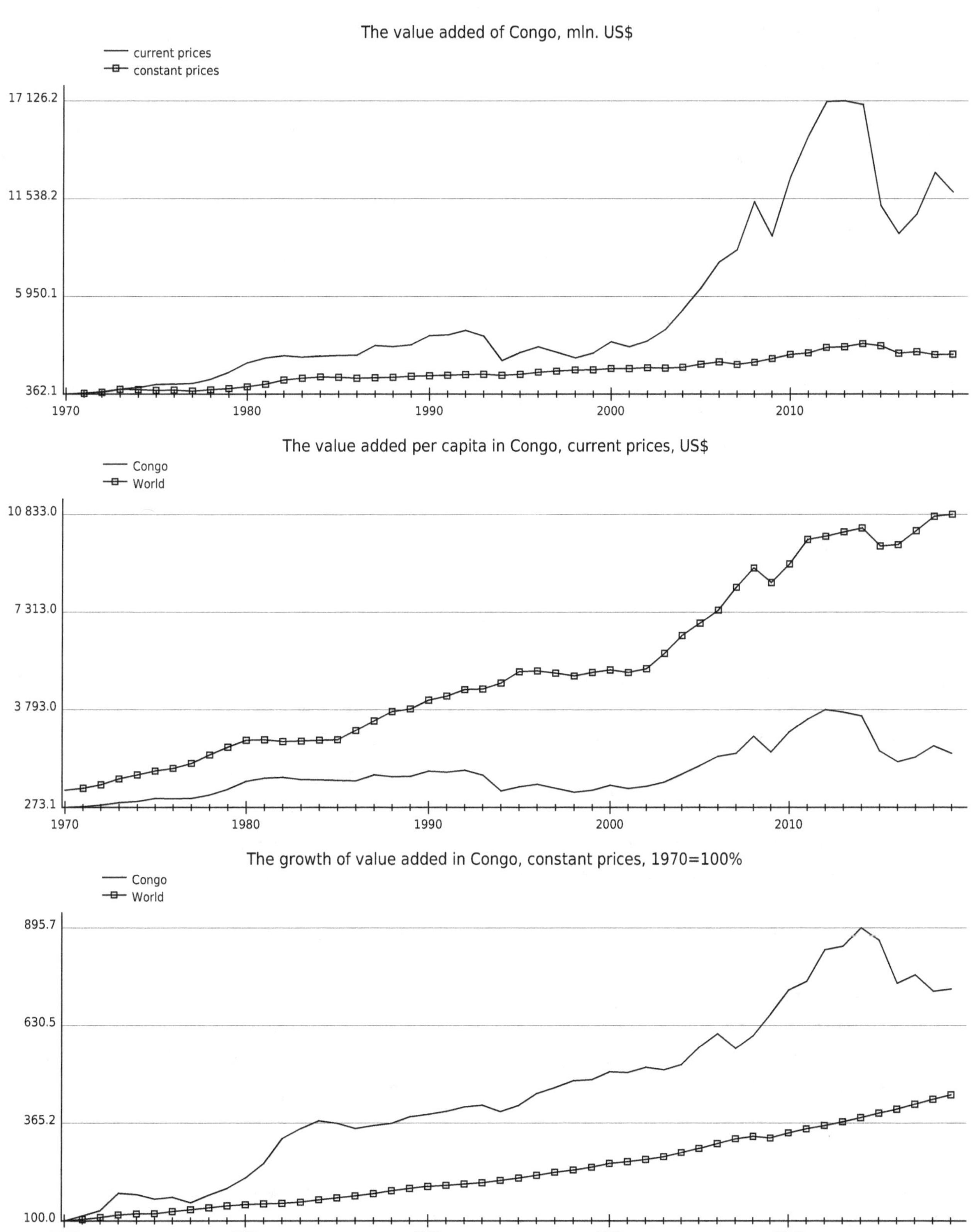

The value added of Congo, mln. US$

The value added per capita in Congo, current prices, US$

The growth of value added in Congo, constant prices, 1970=100%

The 1970s

The value added of Congo was $829.0 million per year in the 1970s, ranked 119th in the world, and was on a par with Haiti ($844.7 million). The share in the world was 0.013%, and 0.33% in Africa.

The total value added of Congo included: services (32.3%), industry (23.5%), agriculture (15.3%), transportation (13.5%), trade (13.1%), and construction (2.3%).

The value added per capita in Congo was $545.7 in the 1970s, ranked 119th in the world, and was on a par with Guinea-Bissau ($537.1). The Congo's value added per capita was less than value added per capita in the world ($1 564.4) in 2.9 times, and was less than value added per capita in Africa ($619.0) by 11.9%.

The growth of value added in Congo was 7.2% in the 1970s, ranked 34th in the world, and was on a par with Thailand (7.2%), Ecuador (7.2%). The growth of value added in Congo (7.2%) was greater than growth of value added in the world (3.9%), was greater than growth of value added in Africa (4.9%).

Comparison with neighbors. The value added of Congo was greater than in the Central African Republic ($565.2 million); but less than in DR Congo ($9.3 billion), in Angola ($4.5 billion), in Cameroon ($3.5 billion), and in Gabon ($2.0 billion). The Congo's value added per capita was greater than in Cameroon ($472.8), in DR Congo ($409.4), and in the Central African Republic ($289.0); but less than in Gabon ($3.1 thousand) and in Angola ($643.9). The growth of value added in Congo was greater than in Cameroon (5.8%), in the Central African Republic (0.80%), in Angola (0.21%), and in DR Congo (0.089%); but less than in Gabon (8.2%).

Comparison with leaders. The value added of Congo was less than in the United States ($1.7 trillion), in the USSR ($649.4 billion), in Japan ($545.3 billion), in Germany ($444.9 billion), and in France ($297.3 billion). The Congo's value added per capita was less than in the United States ($7.8 thousand), in Germany ($5.7 thousand), in France ($5.5 thousand), in Japan ($4.9 thousand), and in the USSR ($2.6 thousand). The growth of value added in Congo was greater than in Japan (4.9%), in the USSR (4.8%), in France (3.7%), in Germany (3.1%), and in the USA (2.9%).

The 1980s

The value added of Congo was $2.7 billion per year in the 1980s, ranked 111th in the world. The share in the world was 0.018%, and 0.52% in Africa.

The total value added of Congo consisted of: industry (30.4%), services (29.1%), trade (14.3%), transportation (13.4%), agriculture (9.8%), and construction (3.0%).

The Congo's value added per capita was $1 314.8 in the 1980s, ranked 100th in the world, and was on a par with Syria ($1 316.0), Micronesia ($1 305.2), Lebanon ($1 297.0). The Congo's value added per capita was less than value added per capita in the world ($3 029.9) in 2.3 times, and was greater than value added per capita in Africa ($948.7) by 38.6%.

The growth of value added in Congo was 7.4% in the 1980s, ranked 13th in the world. The growth of value added in Congo (7.4%) was greater than growth of value added in the world (2.9%), was greater than growth of value added in Africa (1.2%).

Comparison with neighbors. The Congo's value added was greater than in the CAR ($1.1 billion); but less than in DR Congo ($10.4 billion), in Cameroon ($10.3 billion), in Angola ($8.4 billion), and in Gabon ($4.3 billion). The value added per capita in Congo was greater than in Cameroon ($1 032.0), in Angola ($855.6), in the CAR ($449.1), and in DR Congo ($349.6); but less than in Gabon ($5.3 thousand). The growth of value added in Congo was greater than in Cameroon (2.7%), in Angola (2.3%), in DR Congo (1.9%), in the CAR (1.7%), and in Gabon (1.6%).

Comparison with leaders. The value added of Congo was less than in the USA ($4.2 trillion), in Japan ($1.8 trillion), in Germany ($907.0 billion), in the USSR ($887.0 billion), and in France ($650.9 billion). The value added per capita in Congo was less than in the United States ($17.4 thousand), in Japan ($14.8 thousand), in Germany ($11.6 thousand), in France ($11.5 thousand), and in the USSR ($3.2 thousand). The growth of value added in Congo was greater than in the USSR (4.3%), in Japan (4.2%), in the USA (2.8%), in France (2.2%), and in Germany (2.0%).

The 1990s

The value added of Congo was $3.1 billion per year in the 1990s, ranked 131st in the world, and was on a par with New Caledonia ($3.1 billion), Burkina Faso ($3.1 billion). The share in the world was 0.011%, and 0.55% in Africa.

The total value added of Congo consisted of: industry (32.8%), services (29.1%), trade (14.2%), transportation (12.3%), agriculture (10.4%), and construction (1.2%).

The value added per capita in Congo was $1 159.8 in the 1990s, ranked 128th in the world, and was on a par with Tuvalu ($1 155.3), Ukraine ($1 177.9), South-Eastern Asia ($1 185.5). The Congo's value added per capita was less than value added per capita in the world ($4 799.9) in 4.1 times, and was greater than value added per capita in Africa ($793.2) by 46.2%.

The growth of value added in Congo was 2.4% in the 1990s, ranked 121st in the world, and was on a par with Kuwait (2.4%), Tonga (2.4%), Mauritania (2.4%). The growth of value added in Congo (2.4%) was less than growth of value added in the world (2.7%), was greater than growth of value added in Africa (2.3%).

Comparison with neighbors. The value added of Congo was greater than in the CAR ($1.2 billion); but less than in Angola ($11.6 billion), in DR Congo ($11.3 billion), in Cameroon ($10.5 billion), and in Gabon ($5.3 billion). The Congo's value added per capita was greater than in Angola ($841.1), in Cameroon ($783.0), in the CAR ($383.1), and in DR Congo ($278.5); but less than in Gabon ($4.9 thousand). The growth of value added in Congo was greater than in Gabon (2.2%), in the Central African Republic (1.1%), in Cameroon (0.57%), in Angola (-0.78%), and in DR Congo (-5.1%).

Comparison with leaders. The Congo's value added was less than in the USA ($7.6 trillion), in Japan ($4.3 trillion), in Germany ($2.0 trillion), in France ($1.3 trillion), and in the UK ($1.2 trillion). The value added per capita in Congo was less than in Japan ($34.2 thousand), in the United States ($28.6 thousand), in Germany ($24.5 thousand), in France ($21.6 thousand), and in the UK ($21.4 thousand). The growth of value added in Congo was greater than in Germany (2.1%), in France (1.8%), and in Japan (1.8%); but less than in the United States (2.8%) and in the UK (2.4%).

The 2000s

The Congo's value added was $6.3 billion per year in the 2000s, ranked 127th in the world, and was on a par with Afghanistan ($6.2 billion), Georgia ($6.4 billion), Madagascar ($6.4 billion). The share in the world was 0.014%, and 0.59% in Africa.

The total value added of Congo consisted of: industry (53.4%), services (17.5%), trade (9.4%), transportation (8.9%), agriculture (5.5%), and construction (5.4%).

The value added per capita in Congo was $1 743.5 in the 2000s, ranked 139th in the world, and was on a par with Kosovo ($1 756.3), Armenia ($1 715.8), Syria ($1 712.8). The Congo's value added per capita was less than value added per capita in the world ($6 818.0) in 3.9 times, and was greater than value added per capita in Africa ($1 165.9) by 49.5%.

The growth of value added in Congo was 3.2% in the 2000s, ranked 122nd in the world, and was on a par with Saint Vincent (3.2%), Moldova (3.2%), Nicaragua (3.2%). The growth of value added in Congo (3.2%) was greater than growth of value added in the world (2.9%), was less than growth of value added in Africa (4.9%).

Comparison with neighbors. The value added of Congo was greater than in the Central African Republic ($1.4 billion); but less than in Angola ($39.5 billion), in Cameroon ($16.3 billion), in DR Congo ($12.1 billion), and in Gabon ($8.6 billion). The value added per capita in Congo was greater than in Cameroon ($929.5), in the CAR ($343.4), and in DR Congo ($223.3); but less than in Gabon ($6.2 thousand) and in Angola ($2.1 thousand). The growth of value added in Congo was greater than in DR Congo (3.0%), in the CAR (0.67%), and in Gabon (-0.78%); but less than in Angola (8.0%) and in Cameroon (4.3%).

Comparison with leaders. The Congo's value added was less than in the United States ($12.6 trillion), in Japan ($4.7 trillion), in China ($2.6 trillion), in Germany ($2.5 trillion), and in the UK ($2.1 trillion). The Congo's value added per capita was less than in the United States ($42.8 thousand), in Japan ($36.4 thousand), in the United Kingdom ($34.6 thousand), in Germany ($30.7 thousand), and in China ($1 954.1). The growth of value added in Congo was greater than in the United States (1.7%), in the UK (1.7%), in Germany (0.65%), and in Japan (0.27%); but less than in China (10.2%).

The 2010s

The Congo's value added was $13.5 billion per year in the 2010s, ranked 124th in the world. The share in the world was 0.018%, and 0.61% in Africa.

The total value added of Congo included: industry (47.4%), services (18.9%), trade (11.0%), construction (10.3%), transportation (7.0%), and agriculture (5.5%).

The value added per capita in Congo was $2 814.0 in the 2010s, ranked 144th in the world, and was on a par with the Philippines ($2.8 thousand), Vanuatu ($2.8 thousand), Morocco ($2.8 thousand). The value added per capita in Congo was less than value added per capita in the world ($10 094.6) in 3.6 times, and was greater than value added per capita in Africa ($1 886.4) by 49.2%.

The growth of value added in Congo was 1% in the 2010s, ranked 178th in the world, and was on a par with Suriname (1.00%). The growth of value added in Congo (1.0%) was less than growth of value added in the world (3.1%), was less than growth of value added in Africa (2.7%).

Comparison with neighbors. The value added of Congo was 6.8 times higher than in the CAR ($2.0 billion); but 8.4 times lower than in Angola ($113.8 billion), 2.5 times lower than in DR Congo ($33.6 billion), 2.2 times lower than in Cameroon ($30.4 billion), and 11.0% lower than in Gabon ($15.2 billion). The value added per capita in Congo was 2.1 times higher than in Cameroon ($1 320.1), 6.3 times higher than in DR Congo ($446.6), and 6.4 times higher than in the CAR ($438.8); but 2.8 times lower than in Gabon ($8.0 thousand) and 32.0% lower than in Angola ($4.1 thousand). The growth of value added in Congo was greater than in the CAR (-1.7%); but less than in DR Congo (6.3%), in Cameroon (4.4%), in Gabon (4.1%), and in Angola (2.4%).

Comparison with leaders. The Congo's value added was 1 326.7 times lower than in the USA ($18.0 trillion), 776.0 times lower than in China ($10.5 trillion), 384.2 times lower than in Japan ($5.2 trillion), 244.0 times lower than in Germany ($3.3 trillion), and 182.5 times lower than in the UK ($2.5 trillion). The value added per capita in Congo was 20.0 times lower than in the United States ($56.2 thousand), 14.4 times lower than in Japan ($40.7 thousand), 14.3 times lower than in Germany ($40.3 thousand), 13.4 times lower than in the UK ($37.7 thousand), and 2.7 times lower than in China ($7.5 thousand). The growth of value added in Congo was less than in China (7.7%), in the United States (2.2%), in Germany (1.9%), in the United Kingdom (1.8%), and in Japan (1.3%).

Chapter III. Gross national income

The gross national income of Congo rose from $632.2 million per year in the 1970s to $12.0 billion per year in the 2010s, that is by $11.4 billion or 19.0 times. The change occurred at $9.5 billion due to a 4.8-fold increase in prices, as also at $477.6 million due to a 1.2-fold increase in productivity, as well as at $1.4 billion due to the growth in population. The average annual growth in GNI is 3.1%. The minimum value of GNI was in 1970 at $285.1 million. The maximum value of gross national income was in 2014 at $15.7 billion.

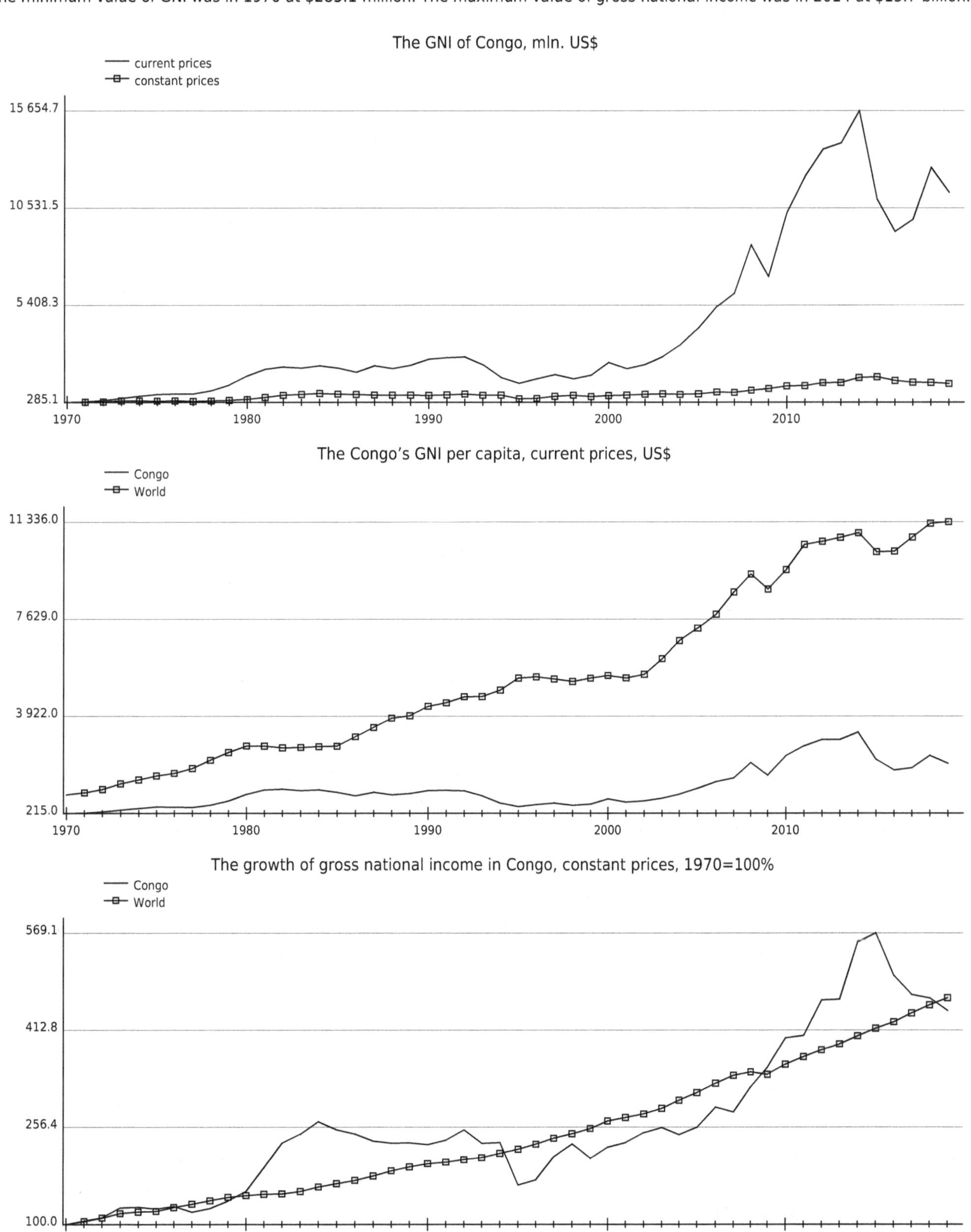

The 1970s

The Congo's gross national income was $632.2 million per year in the 1970s, ranked 128th in the world, and was on a par with Mauritius ($628.9 million), Monaco ($637.7 million), Togo ($639.9 million). The share in the world was 0.0096%, and 0.24% in Africa.

The GNI per capita in Congo was $416.1 in the 1970s, ranked 139th in the world, and was on a par with the Maldives ($414.0), the Philippines ($419.1), Bolivia ($419.7). The gross national income per capita in Congo was less than gross national income per capita in the world ($1 624.3) in 3.9 times, and was less than GNI per capita in Africa ($632.4) by 34.2%.

The growth of gross national income in Congo was 3.6% in the 1970s, ranked 117th in the world, and was on a par with Dominica (3.6%). The growth of gross national income in Congo (3.6%) was less than growth of gross national income in the world (4.1%), was less than growth of gross national income in Africa (4.7%).

Comparison with neighbors. The Congo's gross national income was greater than in the Central African Republic ($397.7 million); but less than in DR Congo ($9.6 billion), in Angola ($4.3 billion), in Cameroon ($3.6 billion), and in Gabon ($2.0 billion). The GNI per capita in Congo was greater than in the Central African Republic ($203.3); but less than in Gabon ($3.0 thousand), in Angola ($617.3), in Cameroon ($489.0), and in DR Congo ($421.3). The growth of GNI in Congo was greater than in the Central African Republic (1.0%), in DR Congo (0.18%), and in Angola (0.14%); but less than in Gabon (7.3%) and in Cameroon (7.2%).

Comparison with leaders. The gross national income of Congo was less than in the USA ($1.7 trillion), in the USSR ($649.4 billion), in Japan ($558.5 billion), in Germany ($486.2 billion), and in France ($334.3 billion). The Congo's GNI per capita was less than in the USA ($7.8 thousand), in France ($6.2 thousand), in Germany ($6.2 thousand), in Japan ($5.0 thousand), and in the USSR ($2.6 thousand). The growth of GNI in Congo was greater than in the USA (3.5%) and in Germany (3.0%); but less than in the USSR (4.8%), in Japan (4.7%), and in France (3.9%).

The 1980s

The Congo's gross national income was $2.1 billion per year in the 1980s, ranked 117th in the world, and was on a par with French Polynesia ($2.1 billion), Malawi ($2.1 billion). The share in the world was 0.014%, and 0.40% in Africa.

The Congo's GNI per capita was $1 015.4 in the 1980s, ranked 116th in the world, and was on a par with Mauritania ($1 029.2). The gross national income per capita in Congo was less than GNI per capita in the world ($3 117.1) in 3.1 times, and was greater than GNI per capita in Africa ($957.8) by 6.0%.

The growth of gross national income in Congo was 5.3% in the 1980s, ranked 34th in the world, and was on a par with French Polynesia (5.3%), the Marshall Islands (5.3%). The growth of gross national income in Congo (5.3%) was greater than growth of gross national income in the world (3.0%), was greater than growth of gross national income in Africa (1.6%).

Comparison with neighbors. The GNI of Congo was greater than in the Central African Republic ($952.2 million); but less than in Cameroon ($10.6 billion), in DR Congo ($10.4 billion), in Angola ($8.0 billion), and in Gabon ($4.2 billion). The GNI per capita in Congo was greater than in Angola ($810.4), in the Central African Republic ($382.1), and in DR Congo ($350.5); but less than in Gabon ($5.2 thousand) and in Cameroon ($1 063.6). The growth of GNI in Congo was greater than in the Central African Republic (3.8%), in Cameroon (2.4%), in Gabon (2.3%), in Angola (2.2%), and in DR Congo (1.2%).

Comparison with leaders. The gross national income of Congo was less than in the United States ($4.2 trillion), in Japan ($1.8 trillion), in Germany ($996.5 billion), in the USSR ($887.0 billion), and in France ($732.1 billion). The Congo's GNI per capita was less than in the USA ($17.4 thousand), in Japan ($15.0 thousand), in France ($13.0 thousand), in Germany ($12.8 thousand), and in the USSR ($3.2 thousand). The growth of GNI in Congo was greater than in Japan (4.4%), in the USSR (4.3%), in the United States (3.1%), in France (2.3%), and in Germany (2.0%).

The 1990s

The Congo's gross national income was $1.9 billion per year in the 1990s, ranked 151st in the world. The share in the world was 0.0068%, and 0.34% in Africa.

The gross national income per capita in Congo was $726.0 in the 1990s, ranked 155th in the world, and was on a par with Albania ($714.3). The GNI per capita in Congo was less than gross national income per capita in the world ($4 991.4) in 6.9 times, and was less than GNI per capita in Africa ($799.7) by 9.2%.

The growth of GNI in Congo was -1.1% in the 1990s, ranked 176th in the world. The growth of gross national income in Congo (-1.1%) was less than growth of GNI in the world (2.8%), was less than growth of GNI in Africa (2.5%).

Comparison with neighbors. The GNI of Congo was greater than in the Central African Republic ($1.2 billion); but less than in DR Congo ($10.5 billion), in Cameroon ($10.4 billion), in Angola ($8.5 billion), and in Gabon ($4.9 billion). The Congo's GNI per capita was greater than in Angola ($615.5), in the CAR ($368.8), and in DR Congo ($259.4); but less than in Gabon ($4.6 thousand) and in Cameroon ($778.3). The growth of gross national income in Congo was greater than in DR Congo (-5.3%); but less than in the CAR (1.8%), in Cameroon (0.42%), in Gabon (0.28%), and in Angola (-0.52%).

Comparison with leaders. The Congo's gross national income was less than in the United States ($7.5 trillion), in Japan ($4.4 trillion), in Germany ($2.2 trillion), in France ($1.4 trillion), and in the United Kingdom ($1.3 trillion). The Congo's gross national income per capita was less than in Japan ($34.7 thousand), in the USA ($28.5 thousand), in Germany ($27.0 thousand), in France ($24.3 thousand), and in the UK ($23.0 thousand). The growth of GNI in Congo was less than in the USA (3.4%), in France (2.2%), in the United Kingdom (2.0%), in Germany (2.0%), and in Japan (1.5%).

The 2000s

The Congo's gross national income was $4.4 billion per year in the 2000s, ranked 146th in the world, and was on a par with Niger ($4.5 billion), Haiti ($4.5 billion). The share in the world was 0.0094%, and 0.41% in Africa.

The gross national income per capita in Congo was $1 215.8 in the 2000s, ranked 154th in the world, and was on a par with Nigeria ($1 229.8). The GNI per capita in Congo was less than gross national income per capita in the world ($7 165.2) in 5.9 times, and was greater than gross national income per capita in Africa ($1 185.1) by 2.6%.

The growth of GNI in Congo was 5.5% in the 2000s, ranked 44th in the world, and was on a par with Cuba (5.5%), Albania (5.5%), Indonesia (5.5%). The growth of GNI in Congo (5.5%) was greater than growth of gross national income in the world (3.0%), was greater than growth of GNI in Africa (5.1%).

Comparison with neighbors. The GNI of Congo was greater than in the Central African Republic ($1.4 billion); but less than in Angola ($34.3 billion), in Cameroon ($17.2 billion), in DR Congo ($12.2 billion), and in Gabon ($7.3 billion). The Congo's gross national income per capita was greater than in Cameroon ($980.1), in the CAR ($351.3), and in DR Congo ($224.9); but less than in Gabon ($5.3 thousand) and in Angola ($1 780.2). The growth of GNI in Congo was greater than in Cameroon (4.4%), in DR Congo (3.2%), in Gabon (1.5%), and in the Central African Republic (1.4%); but less than in Angola (10.1%).

Comparison with leaders. The gross national income of Congo was less than in the United States ($12.7 trillion), in Japan ($4.8 trillion), in Germany ($2.8 trillion), in China ($2.6 trillion), and in the United Kingdom ($2.3 trillion). The GNI per capita in Congo was less than in the United States ($43.2 thousand), in the United Kingdom ($38.5 thousand), in Japan ($37.1 thousand), in Germany ($34.2 thousand), and in China ($1 950.5). The growth of GNI in Congo was greater than in the USA (1.8%), in the United Kingdom (1.7%), in Germany (1.0%), and in Japan (0.62%); but less than in China (10.4%).

The 2010s

The Congo's GNI was $12.0 billion per year in the 2010s, ranked 132nd in the world, and was on a par with Namibia ($12.0 billion), Madagascar ($11.9 billion), Chad ($11.8 billion). The share in the world was 0.015%, and 0.54% in Africa.

The gross national income per capita in Congo was $2 493.3 in the 2010s, ranked 154th in the world, and was on a par with Papua New Guinea ($2.5 thousand), Moldova ($2.4 thousand). The GNI per capita in Congo was less than GNI per capita in the world ($10 611.7) in 4.3 times, and was greater than gross national income per capita in Africa ($1 913.3) by 30.3%.

The growth of gross national income in Congo was 2.3% in the 2010s, ranked 134th in the world. The growth of gross national income in Congo (2.3%) was less than growth of gross national income in the world (3.1%), was less than growth of GNI in Africa (2.9%).

Comparison with neighbors. The Congo's gross national income was 5.7 times higher than in the CAR ($2.1 billion); but 8.8 times lower than in Angola ($105.5 billion), 2.9 times lower than in DR Congo ($34.5 billion), 2.7 times lower than in Cameroon ($32.3 billion), and 19.2% lower than in Gabon ($14.8 billion). The GNI per capita in Congo was 77.9% higher than in Cameroon ($1 401.2), 5.3 times higher than in the Central African Republic ($468.0), and 5.4 times higher than in DR Congo ($458.4); but 3.1 times lower than in Gabon ($7.8 thousand) and 35.0% lower than in Angola ($3.8 thousand). The growth of gross national income in Congo was greater than in the CAR (-0.82%); but less than in DR Congo (6.5%), in Gabon (4.6%), in Cameroon (4.4%), and in Angola (2.7%).

Comparison with leaders. The Congo's GNI was 1 526.2 times lower than in the USA ($18.3 trillion), 872.6 times lower than in China ($10.5 trillion), 450.1 times lower than in Japan ($5.4 trillion), 312.6 times lower than in Germany ($3.7 trillion), and 228.9 times lower than in France ($2.7 trillion). The gross national income per capita in Congo was 23.0 times lower than in the United States ($57.3 thousand), 18.4 times lower than in Germany ($45.8 thousand), 16.9 times lower than in Japan ($42.2 thousand), 16.6 times lower than in France ($41.4 thousand), and 3.0 times lower than in China ($7.5 thousand). The growth of GNI in Congo was greater than in Germany (2.0%), in Japan (1.4%), and in France (1.4%); but less than in China (7.7%) and in the United States (2.5%).

Part II. Structure

The 2010s
agriculture   5.5%
industry   47.4%
construction   10.3%
trade   11.0%
transportation   7.0%
services   18.9%

Chapter IV. Agriculture

Agriculture, hunting, forestry, fishing (ISIC A-B)

The agriculture of Congo increased from $126.6 million per year in the 1970s to $747.2 million per year in the 2010s, that is by $620.6 million or 5.9 times. The change occurred at $365.9 million due to a 2.0-fold increase in prices, as also at -$19.7 million due to a 1.1-fold decrease in productivity, as well as at $274.3 million due to the expansion in population. The average annual growth in agriculture is 2.6%. The minimum value of agriculture was in 1970 at $72.1 million. The maximum value of agriculture was in 2018 at $939.2 million.

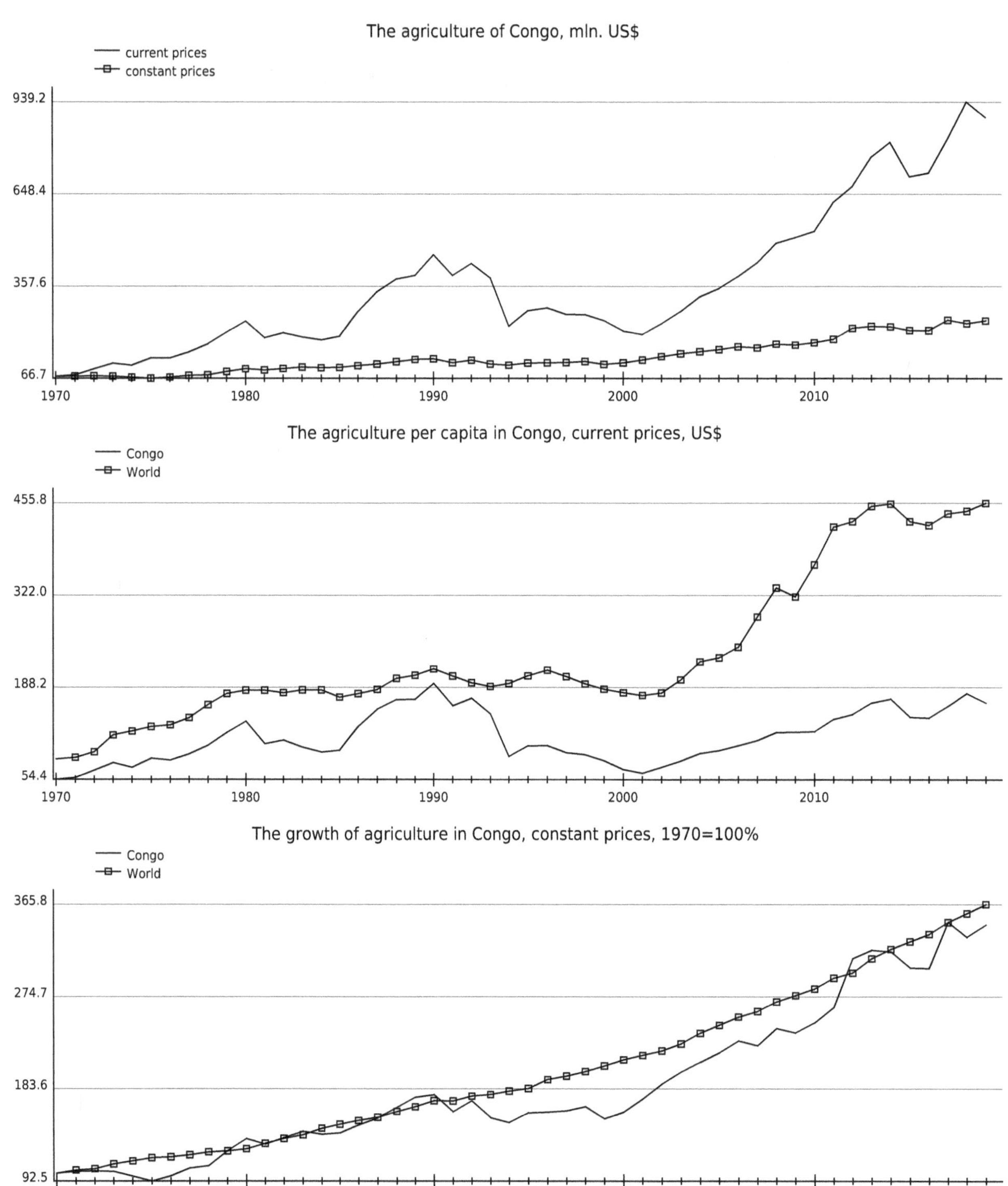

The agriculture of Congo, mln. US$

The agriculture per capita in Congo, current prices, US$

The growth of agriculture in Congo, constant prices, 1970=100%

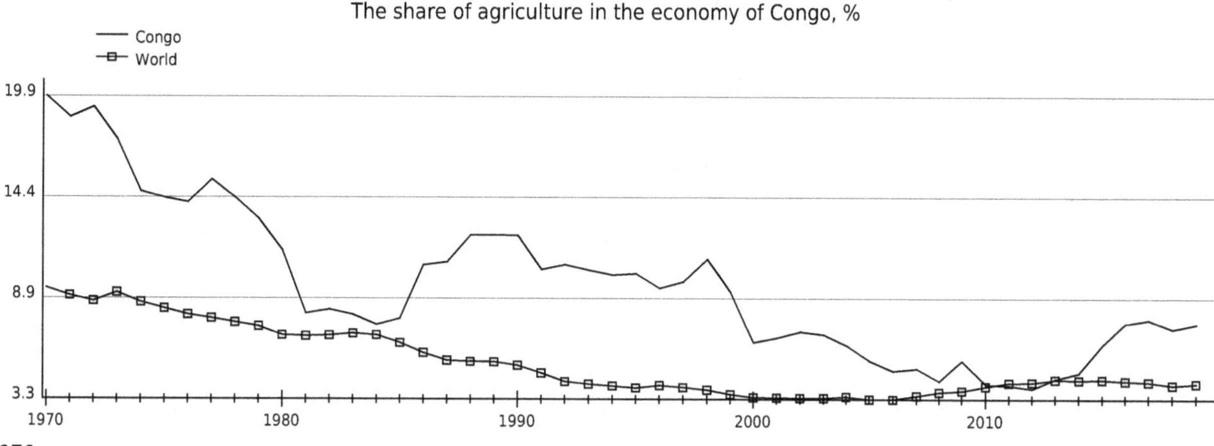

The 1970s

The agriculture of Congo was $126.6 million per year in the 1970s, ranked 120th in the world, and was on a par with Lebanon ($127.4 million). The share in the world was 0.025%, and 0.27% in Africa.

The share of agriculture in the economy of Congo was 15.3% in the 1970s, ranked 94th in the world, and was on a par with Nigeria (15.3%), Northern Africa (15.3%), Costa Rica (15.4%).

The Congo's agriculture per capita was $83.3 in the 1970s, ranked 123rd in the world, and was on a par with Saint Lucia ($83.4), the Seychelles ($83.6), Malta ($82.8). The sector of agriculture per capita in Congo was less than agriculture per capita in the world ($127.6) by 34.7%, and was less than agriculture per capita in Africa ($112.2) by 25.7%.

The growth of agriculture in Congo was 2.2% in the 1970s, ranked 106th in the world, and was on a par with the World (2.2%), Northern Africa (2.2%). The growth of agriculture in Congo (2.2%) was less than growth of agriculture in the world (2.2%), was greater than growth of agriculture in Africa (1.7%).

Comparison with neighbors. The value added of agriculture in Congo was greater than in Gabon ($111.9 million); but less than in DR Congo ($2.2 billion), in Cameroon ($713.0 million), in Angola ($640.2 million), and in the Central African Republic ($180.3 million). The Congo's agriculture per capita was less than in Gabon ($173.7), in Cameroon ($96.5), in DR Congo ($96.0), in Angola ($92.6), and in the Central African Republic ($92.2). The growth of agriculture in Congo was greater than in DR Congo (1.6%) and in Angola (0.32%); but less than in Gabon (8.1%), in Cameroon (5.5%), and in the Central African Republic (2.3%).

Comparison with leaders. The agriculture of Congo was less than in the USSR ($88.7 billion), in China ($49.5 billion), in the United States ($42.6 billion), in India ($36.0 billion), and in Japan ($25.8 billion). The value of agriculture per capita in Congo was greater than in India ($58.3) and in China ($54.2); but less than in the USSR ($351.8), in Japan ($231.3), and in the USA ($195.0). The growth of agriculture in Congo was greater than in Japan (0.52%), in the USA (0.34%), and in India (0.30%); but less than in the USSR (7.0%) and in China (2.4%).

The 1980s

The value added of agriculture in Congo was $262.7 million per year in the 1980s, ranked 117th in the world, and was on a par with Gabon ($263.6 million), Gambia ($259.6 million). The share in the world was 0.029%, and 0.30% in Africa.

The share of agriculture in the economy of Congo was 9.8% in the 1980s, ranked 109th in the world, and was on a par with Brazil (9.8%).

The value added of agriculture per capita in Congo was $129.4 in the 1980s, ranked 123rd in the world, and was on a par with Zimbabwe ($129.4), Montserrat ($129.3), Angola ($129.5). The value of agriculture per capita in Congo was less than agriculture per capita in the world ($186.6) by 30.6%, and was less than agriculture per capita in Africa ($159.2) by 18.7%.

The growth of agriculture in Congo was 3.7% in the 1980s, ranked 50th in the world, and was on a par with Somalia (3.6%), Brunei (3.6%), the United States (3.7%). The growth of agriculture in Congo (3.7%) was greater than growth of agriculture in the world (3.1%), was greater than growth of agriculture in Africa (2.8%).

Comparison with neighbors. The Congo's agriculture was less than in DR Congo ($3.1 billion), in Cameroon ($1.6 billion), in Angola

($1.3 billion), in the CAR ($390.2 million), and in Gabon ($263.6 million). The value added of agriculture per capita in Congo was greater than in DR Congo ($104.8); but less than in Gabon ($321.6), in Cameroon ($162.5), in the CAR ($156.6), and in Angola ($129.5). The growth of agriculture in Congo was greater than in Cameroon (3.1%), in DR Congo (2.6%), in the Central African Republic (1.9%), in Gabon (1.3%), and in Angola (0.71%).

Comparison with leaders. The value added of agriculture in Congo was less than in the USSR ($125.8 billion), in China ($94.9 billion), in India ($70.4 billion), in the United States ($68.7 billion), and in Japan ($49.7 billion). The agriculture per capita in Congo was greater than in India ($90.7) and in China ($88.5); but less than in the USSR ($457.2), in Japan ($410.0), and in the USA ($286.8). The growth of agriculture in Congo was greater than in the USSR (2.8%) and in Japan (0.41%); but less than in China (5.3%), in India (4.4%), and in the USA (3.7%).

The 1990s

The Congo's agriculture was $324.6 million per year in the 1990s, ranked 139th in the world, and was on a par with Namibia ($318.0 million). The share in the world was 0.029%, and 0.34% in Africa.

The share of agriculture in the economy of Congo was 10.4% in the 1990s, ranked 112th in the world.

The Congo's agriculture per capita was $121.1 in the 1990s, ranked 158th in the world, and was on a par with Mali ($122.6), Cambodia ($123.2), Malawi ($118.3). The value of agriculture per capita in Congo was less than agriculture per capita in the world ($199.8) by 39.4%, and was less than agriculture per capita in Africa ($134.5) by 10.0%.

The growth of agriculture in Congo was -1.3% in the 1990s, ranked 166th in the world. The growth of agriculture in Congo (-1.3%) was less than growth of agriculture in the world (2.2%), was less than growth of agriculture in Africa (2.8%).

Comparison with neighbors. The agriculture of Congo was less than in DR Congo ($5.2 billion), in Cameroon ($1.8 billion), in Angola ($1.5 billion), in the Central African Republic ($456.5 million), and in Gabon ($372.9 million). The value of agriculture per capita in Congo was greater than in Angola ($109.9); but less than in Gabon ($347.7), in the CAR ($143.6), in Cameroon ($131.6), and in DR Congo ($129.1). The growth of agriculture in Congo was greater than in Angola (-3.7%); but less than in the CAR (3.1%), in Gabon (2.3%), in DR Congo (2.1%), and in Cameroon (0.66%).

Comparison with leaders. The sector of agriculture in Congo was less than in China ($139.0 billion), in the USA ($96.1 billion), in India ($91.4 billion), in Japan ($78.9 billion), and in Brazil ($36.8 billion). The value of agriculture per capita in Congo was greater than in China ($112.7) and in India ($95.6); but less than in Japan ($625.5), in the United States ($363.4), and in Brazil ($228.7). The growth of agriculture in Congo was greater than in Japan (-1.8%); but less than in China (4.3%), in Brazil (3.0%), in India (2.8%), and in the USA (2.6%).

The 2000s

The value added of agriculture in Congo was $343.9 million per year in the 2000s, ranked 145th in the world, and was on a par with Gambia ($337.1 million). The share in the world was 0.022%, and 0.21% in Africa.

The share of agriculture in the economy of Congo was 5.5% in the 2000s, ranked 125th in the world, and was on a par with Iraq (5.5%), Mauritius (5.4%).

The agriculture per capita in Congo was $95.6 in the 2000s, ranked 189th in the world, and was on a par with Montserrat ($95.9), Guinea ($95.2), Mozambique ($97.4). The Congo's agriculture per capita was less than agriculture per capita in the world ($240.3) in 2.5 times, and was less than agriculture per capita in Africa ($182.0) by 47.5%.

The growth of agriculture in Congo was 4.5% in the 2000s, ranked 35th in the world, and was on a par with Ghana (4.5%), Benin (4.5%), Tanzania (4.5%). The growth of agriculture in Congo (4.5%) was greater than growth of agriculture in the world (3.0%), was less than growth of agriculture in Africa (5.1%).

Comparison with neighbors. The Congo's agriculture was less than in DR Congo ($3.1 billion), in Cameroon ($2.5 billion), in Angola ($2.2 billion), in the Central African Republic ($593.3 million), and in Gabon ($455.0 million). The value added of agriculture per capita in Congo was greater than in DR Congo ($56.5); but less than in Gabon ($329.0), in the CAR ($148.4), in Cameroon ($139.6), and in Angola ($114.6). The growth of agriculture in Congo was greater than in Cameroon (2.9%), in Gabon (2.1%), in the Central African Republic (1.3%), and in DR Congo (-0.12%); but less than in Angola (8.3%).

Comparison with leaders. The Congo's agriculture was less than in China ($297.7 billion), in India ($147.6 billion), in the USA ($122.5 billion), in Japan ($57.1 billion), and in Nigeria ($47.6 billion). The value added of agriculture per capita in Congo was less than in Japan ($445.6), in the USA ($416.9), in Nigeria ($346.4), in China ($224.5), and in India ($129.7). The growth of agriculture in Congo was greater than in China (4.0%), in the United States (3.6%), in India (2.0%), and in Japan (-1.3%); but less than in Nigeria (10.1%).

The 2010s

The value of agriculture in Congo was $747.2 million per year in the 2010s, ranked 139th in the world, and was on a par with Kosovo ($737.6 million). The share in the world was 0.024%, and 0.22% in Africa.

The share of agriculture in the economy of Congo was 5.5% in the 2010s, ranked 120th in the world, and was on a par with Eastern Asia (5.5%), Venezuela (5.6%), Costa Rica (5.6%).

The sector of agriculture per capita in Congo was $155.3 in the 2010s, ranked 180th in the world, and was on a par with the CAR ($155.5), Southern Africa ($153.9), Trinidad and Tobago ($158.5). The value of agriculture per capita in Congo was less than agriculture per capita in the world ($432.1) in 2.8 times, and was less than agriculture per capita in Africa ($294.3) by 47.2%.

The growth of agriculture in Congo was 3.8% in the 2010s, ranked 48th in the world, and was on a par with Azerbaijan (3.7%), Africa (3.7%), Bangladesh (3.8%). The growth of agriculture in Congo (3.8%) was greater than growth of agriculture in the world (2.9%), was greater than growth of agriculture in Africa (3.7%).

Comparison with neighbors. The value of agriculture in Congo was 6.3% higher than in the CAR ($702.8 million) and 8.2% higher than in Gabon ($690.6 million); but 11.9 times lower than in Angola ($8.9 billion), 9.3 times lower than in DR Congo ($7.0 billion), and 6.2 times lower than in Cameroon ($4.7 billion). The value of agriculture per capita in Congo was 67.7% higher than in DR Congo ($92.6); but 2.3 times lower than in Gabon ($362.1), 2.1 times lower than in Angola ($323.6), 23.4% lower than in Cameroon ($202.7), and 0.11% lower than in the CAR ($155.5). The growth of agriculture in Congo was greater than in DR Congo (3.4%) and in the Central African Republic (-3.5%); but less than in Gabon (6.7%), in Angola (5.3%), and in Cameroon (4.7%).

Comparison with leaders. The Congo's agriculture was 1 186.1 times lower than in China ($886.2 billion), 486.4 times lower than in India ($363.4 billion), 241.3 times lower than in the USA ($180.3 billion), 166.0 times lower than in Indonesia ($124.1 billion), and 128.2 times lower than in Nigeria ($95.8 billion). The value of agriculture per capita in Congo was 4.1 times lower than in China ($631.9), 3.6 times lower than in the United States ($564.3), 3.4 times lower than in Nigeria ($534.6), 3.1 times lower than in Indonesia ($483.6), and 44.4% lower than in India ($279.1). The growth of agriculture in Congo was greater than in Nigeria (3.6%) and in the United States (2.0%); but less than in India (4.1%), in Indonesia (3.9%), and in China (3.8%).

Chapter V. Industry

Mining, Manufacturing, Utilities (ISIC C-E)

The value added of industry in Congo increased from $194.5 million per year in the 1970s to $6.4 billion per year in the 2010s, that is by $6.2 billion or 33.0 times. The change occurred at $5.2 billion due to a 5.4-fold increase in prices, as also at $582.1 million due to a 1.9-fold increase in productivity, as well as at $421.5 million due to the growth in population. The average annual growth in industry is 6.3%. The minimum value of industry was in 1970 at $63.2 million. The maximum value of industry was in 2012 at $9.5 billion.

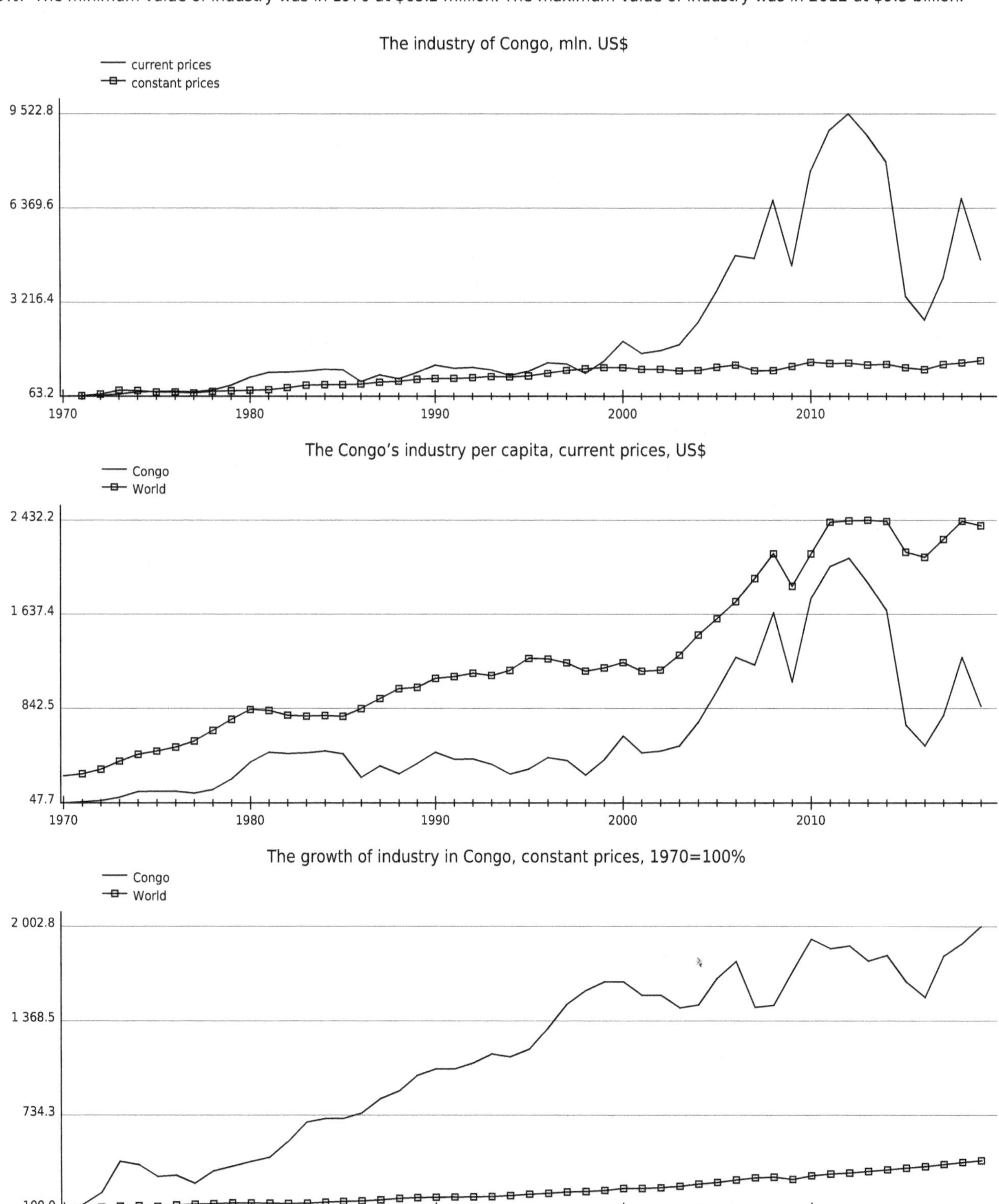

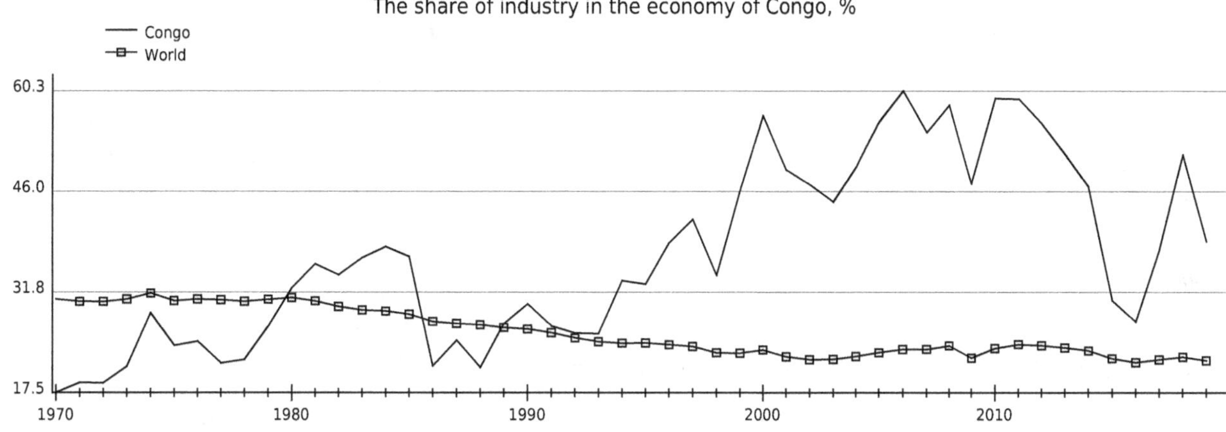

The 1970s

The value added of industry in Congo was $194.5 million per year in the 1970s, ranked 115th in the world, and was on a par with Malawi ($195.0 million), Jordan ($191.4 million), Liberia ($189.9 million). The share in the world was 0.010%, and 0.26% in Africa.

The share of industry in the economy of Congo was 23.5% in the 1970s, ranked 90th in the world, and was on a par with Thailand (23.6%), Guinea (23.3%).

The sector of industry per capita in Congo was $128.1 in the 1970s, ranked 103rd in the world, and was on a par with Tunisia ($127.9), Mauritius ($127.0). The industry per capita in Congo was less than industry per capita in the world ($480.5) in 3.8 times, and was less than industry per capita in Africa ($181.2) by 29.3%.

The growth of industry in Congo was 16.3% in the 1970s, ranked 2nd in the world. The growth of industry in Congo (16.3%) was greater than growth of industry in the world (4.0%), was greater than growth of industry in Africa (5.5%).

Comparison with neighbors. The Congo's industry was greater than in the CAR ($144.5 million); but less than in DR Congo ($2.2 billion), in Angola ($1.6 billion), in Gabon ($876.8 million), and in Cameroon ($492.2 million). The industry per capita in Congo was greater than in DR Congo ($98.7), in the CAR ($73.9), and in Cameroon ($66.6); but less than in Gabon ($1 360.4) and in Angola ($225.9). The growth of industry in Congo was greater than in Gabon (8.1%), in Cameroon (6.2%), in Angola (0.19%), in the Central African Republic (0.022%), and in DR Congo (-0.96%).

Comparison with leaders. The value added of industry in Congo was less than in the United States ($450.4 billion), in the USSR ($248.8 billion), in Japan ($185.6 billion), in Germany ($158.4 billion), and in the UK ($72.6 billion). The sector of industry per capita in Congo was less than in the USA ($2.1 thousand), in Germany ($2.0 thousand), in Japan ($1 666.5), in the UK ($1 295.1), and in the USSR ($986.6). The growth of industry in Congo was greater than in the USSR (5.2%), in Japan (4.5%), in the USA (2.4%), in Germany (2.1%), and in the UK (1.9%).

The 1980s

The industry of Congo was $810.2 million per year in the 1980s, ranked 97th in the world. The share in the world was 0.019%, and 0.52% in Africa.

The share of industry in the economy of Congo was 30.4% in the 1980s, ranked 43rd in the world, and was on a par with Bahrain (30.3%), Africa (30.4%), South-Eastern Asia (30.4%).

The value of industry per capita in Congo was $399.2 in the 1980s, ranked 86th in the world, and was on a par with Montserrat ($397.0). The industry per capita in Congo was less than industry per capita in the world ($861.8) in 2.2 times, and was greater than industry per capita in Africa ($288.5) by 38.4%.

The growth of industry in Congo was 9.9% in the 1980s, ranked 14th in the world. The growth of industry in Congo (9.9%) was greater than growth of industry in the world (2.3%), was greater than growth of industry in Africa (-0.99%).

Comparison with neighbors. The value of industry in Congo was greater than in the Central African Republic ($241.9 million); but less than in Angola ($3.0 billion), in DR Congo ($2.7 billion), in Cameroon ($2.3 billion), and in Gabon ($1.9 billion). The value of industry per capita in Congo was greater than in Angola ($302.5), in Cameroon ($226.5), in the Central African Republic ($97.1), and in DR

Congo ($90.8); but less than in Gabon ($2.3 thousand). The growth of industry in Congo was greater than in Cameroon (4.4%), in Angola (3.4%), in Gabon (1.9%), in DR Congo (1.8%), and in the Central African Republic (1.2%).

Comparison with leaders. The value of industry in Congo was less than in the United States ($1.0 trillion), in Japan ($566.4 billion), in the USSR ($305.7 billion), in Germany ($297.5 billion), and in the UK ($171.2 billion). The sector of industry per capita in Congo was less than in Japan ($4.7 thousand), in the United States ($4.2 thousand), in Germany ($3.8 thousand), in the United Kingdom ($3.0 thousand), and in the USSR ($1 110.8). The growth of industry in Congo was greater than in the USSR (5.3%), in Japan (4.2%), in the United States (1.9%), in the United Kingdom (1.4%), and in Germany (1.2%).

The 1990s

The industry of Congo was $1.0 billion per year in the 1990s, ranked 114th in the world, and was on a par with Cyprus ($1.0 billion), Honduras ($1.0 billion). The share in the world was 0.015%, and 0.65% in Africa.

The share of industry in the economy of Congo was 32.8% in the 1990s, ranked 30th in the world, and was on a par with Indonesia (32.8%), Czechia (32.7%).

The Congo's industry per capita was $380.4 in the 1990s, ranked 105th in the world, and was on a par with Suriname ($378.2), Equatorial Guinea ($376.9), Belize ($387.2). The value of industry per capita in Congo was less than industry per capita in the world ($1 175.6) in 3.1 times, and was greater than industry per capita in Africa ($222.8) by 70.7%.

The growth of industry in Congo was 5% in the 1990s, ranked 54th in the world, and was on a par with Southern Asia (5.0%), Kiribati (5.0%), Panama (5.0%). The growth of industry in Congo (5.0%) was greater than growth of industry in the world (2.5%), was greater than growth of industry in Africa (1.3%).

Comparison with neighbors. The industry of Congo was greater than in the CAR ($280.2 million); but less than in Angola ($5.9 billion), in Gabon ($2.4 billion), in Cameroon ($2.4 billion), and in DR Congo ($1.9 billion). The value added of industry per capita in Congo was greater than in Cameroon ($178.3), in the CAR ($88.1), and in DR Congo ($47.4); but less than in Gabon ($2.3 thousand) and in Angola ($430.7). The growth of industry in Congo was greater than in Angola (2.1%), in Gabon (1.9%), in the Central African Republic (-0.12%), in Cameroon (-0.52%), and in DR Congo (-11.2%).

Comparison with leaders. The sector of industry in Congo was less than in the United States ($1.5 trillion), in Japan ($1.2 trillion), in Germany ($534.0 billion), in China ($285.9 billion), and in the United Kingdom ($268.6 billion). The value added of industry per capita in Congo was greater than in China ($231.9); but less than in Japan ($9.4 thousand), in Germany ($6.6 thousand), in the United States ($5.7 thousand), and in the United Kingdom ($4.6 thousand). The growth of industry in Congo was greater than in the United States (2.8%), in Japan (1.3%), in the UK (1.2%), and in Germany (0.33%); but less than in China (13.1%).

The 2000s

The Congo's industry was $3.3 billion per year in the 2000s, ranked 98th in the world, and was on a par with Melanesia ($3.4 billion), Luxembourg ($3.4 billion), DR Congo ($3.4 billion). The share in the world was 0.033%, and 1.0% in Africa.

The share of industry in the economy of Congo was 53.4% in the 2000s, ranked 11th in the world.

The industry per capita in Congo was $930.5 in the 2000s, ranked 96th in the world, and was on a par with Eswatini ($921.8), Belarus ($942.2), Asia ($951.8). The sector of industry per capita in Congo was less than industry per capita in the world ($1 573.8) by 40.9%, and was greater than industry per capita in Africa ($352.5) in 2.6 times.

The growth of industry in Congo was 0.4% in the 2000s, ranked 164th in the world. The growth of industry in Congo (0.40%) was less than growth of industry in the world (2.9%), was less than growth of industry in Africa (3.1%).

Comparison with neighbors. The value added of industry in Congo was greater than in the CAR ($254.4 million); but less than in Angola ($19.8 billion), in Gabon ($4.8 billion), in Cameroon ($4.1 billion), and in DR Congo ($3.4 billion). The Congo's industry per capita was greater than in Cameroon ($235.5), in the Central African Republic ($63.6), and in DR Congo ($63.0); but less than in Gabon ($3.5 thousand) and in Angola ($1 027.0). The growth of industry in Congo was greater than in Gabon (-5.3%); but less than in Angola (8.7%), in the CAR (3.3%), in DR Congo (3.1%), and in Cameroon (2.4%).

Comparison with leaders. The value added of industry in Congo was less than in the USA ($2.1 trillion), in Japan ($1.1 trillion), in China ($1.1 trillion), in Germany ($629.4 billion), and in the United Kingdom ($345.1 billion). The Congo's industry per capita was greater than in China ($795.3); but less than in Japan ($8.8 thousand), in Germany ($7.7 thousand), in the United States ($7.1 thousand), and in the United Kingdom ($5.7 thousand). The growth of industry in Congo was greater than in Germany (0.19%), in Japan (0.15%), and in the United Kingdom (-1.1%); but less than in China (11.1%) and in the United States (1.5%).

The 2010s

The value added of industry in Congo was $6.4 billion per year in the 2010s, ranked 101st in the world. The share in the world was 0.038%, and 1.1% in Africa.

The share of industry in the economy of Congo was 47.4% in the 2010s, ranked 14th in the world, and was on a par with Azerbaijan (47.6%).

The industry per capita in Congo was $1 333.4 in the 2010s, ranked 97th in the world, and was on a par with Swaziland ($1 312.3), the TCI ($1 310.1), Barbados ($1 366.4). The sector of industry per capita in Congo was less than industry per capita in the world ($2 320.9) by 42.6%, and was greater than industry per capita in Africa ($489.1) in 2.7 times.

The growth of industry in Congo was 1.7% in the 2010s, ranked 143rd in the world, and was on a par with Northern Europe (1.7%). The growth of industry in Congo (1.7%) was less than growth of industry in the world (3.5%), was greater than growth of industry in Africa (0.035%).

Comparison with neighbors. The Congo's industry was 14.8 times higher than in the Central African Republic ($434.5 million); but 6.5 times lower than in Angola ($41.7 billion), 2.2 times lower than in DR Congo ($14.4 billion), 15.4% lower than in Gabon ($7.6 billion), and 9.0% lower than in Cameroon ($7.0 billion). The Congo's industry per capita was 4.4 times higher than in Cameroon ($306.0), 7.0 times higher than in DR Congo ($190.9), and 13.9 times higher than in the Central African Republic ($96.1); but 3.0 times lower than in Gabon ($4.0 thousand) and 12.2% lower than in Angola ($1 518.4). The growth of industry in Congo was greater than in Gabon (0.77%), in Angola (0.33%), and in the Central African Republic (-3.1%); but less than in DR Congo (10.9%) and in Cameroon (3.6%).

Comparison with leaders. The sector of industry in Congo was 574.2 times lower than in China ($3.7 trillion), 427.4 times lower than in the USA ($2.7 trillion), 185.6 times lower than in Japan ($1.2 trillion), 130.9 times lower than in Germany ($840.0 billion), and 69.1 times lower than in India ($443.4 billion). The industry per capita in Congo was 3.9 times higher than in India ($340.6); but 7.7 times lower than in Germany ($10.3 thousand), 7.0 times lower than in Japan ($9.3 thousand), 6.4 times lower than in the United States ($8.6 thousand), and 49.2% lower than in China ($2.6 thousand). The growth of industry in Congo was less than in China (7.5%), in India (6.5%), in Germany (3.2%), in Japan (2.6%), and in the USA (2.2%).

Chapter 5.1. Manufacturing

(ISIC D)

The value of manufacturing in Congo rose from $115.1 million per year in the 1970s to $986.1 million per year in the 2010s, that is by $871.1 million or 8.6 times. The change occurred at $543.2 million due to a 2.2-fold increase in prices, as also at $78.6 million due to a 1.2-fold increase in productivity, as well as at $249.3 million due to the expansion in population. The average annual growth in manufacturing is 2.4%. The minimum value of manufacturing was in 1970 at $59.0 million. The maximum value of manufacturing was in 2017 at $1.2 billion.

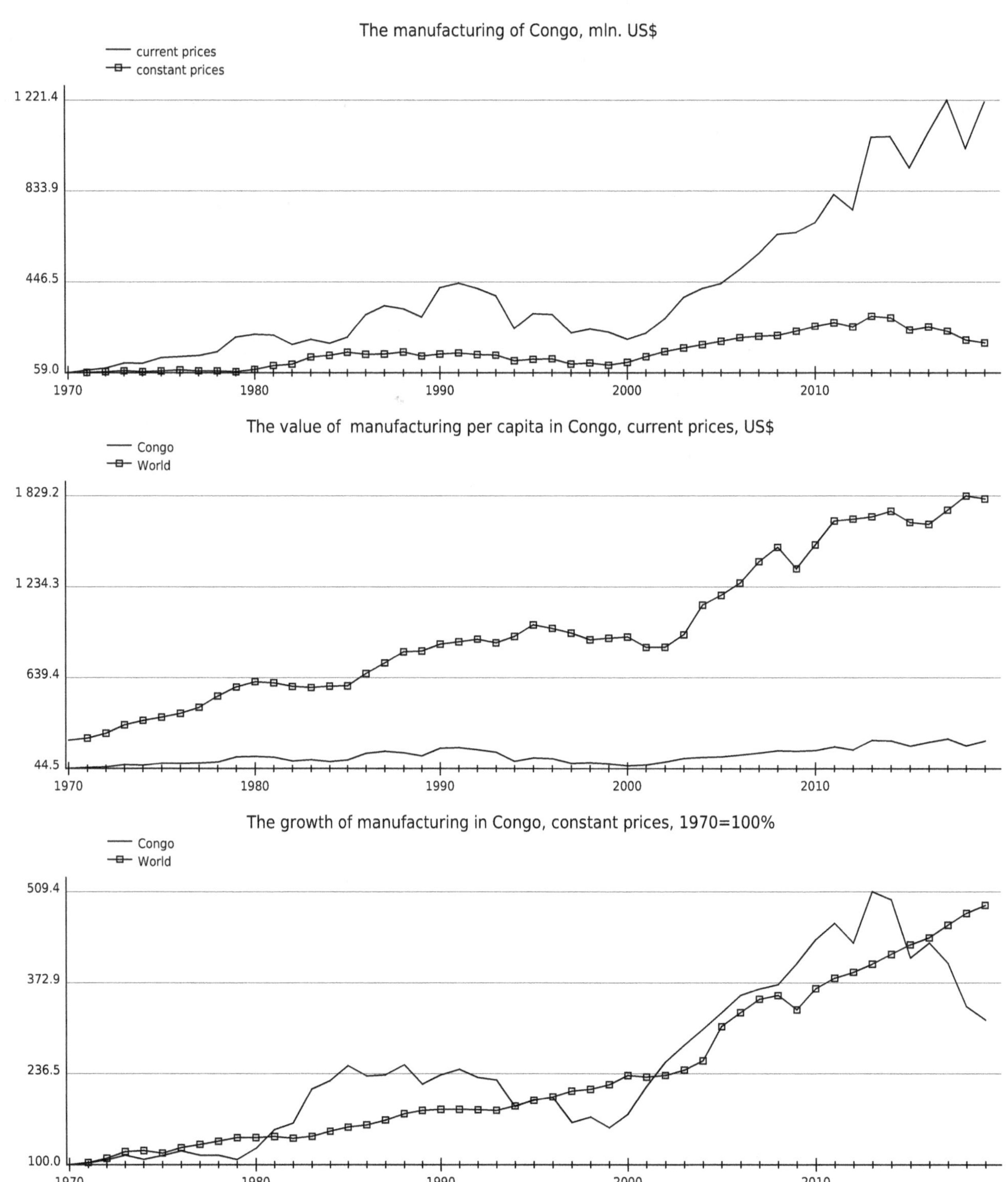

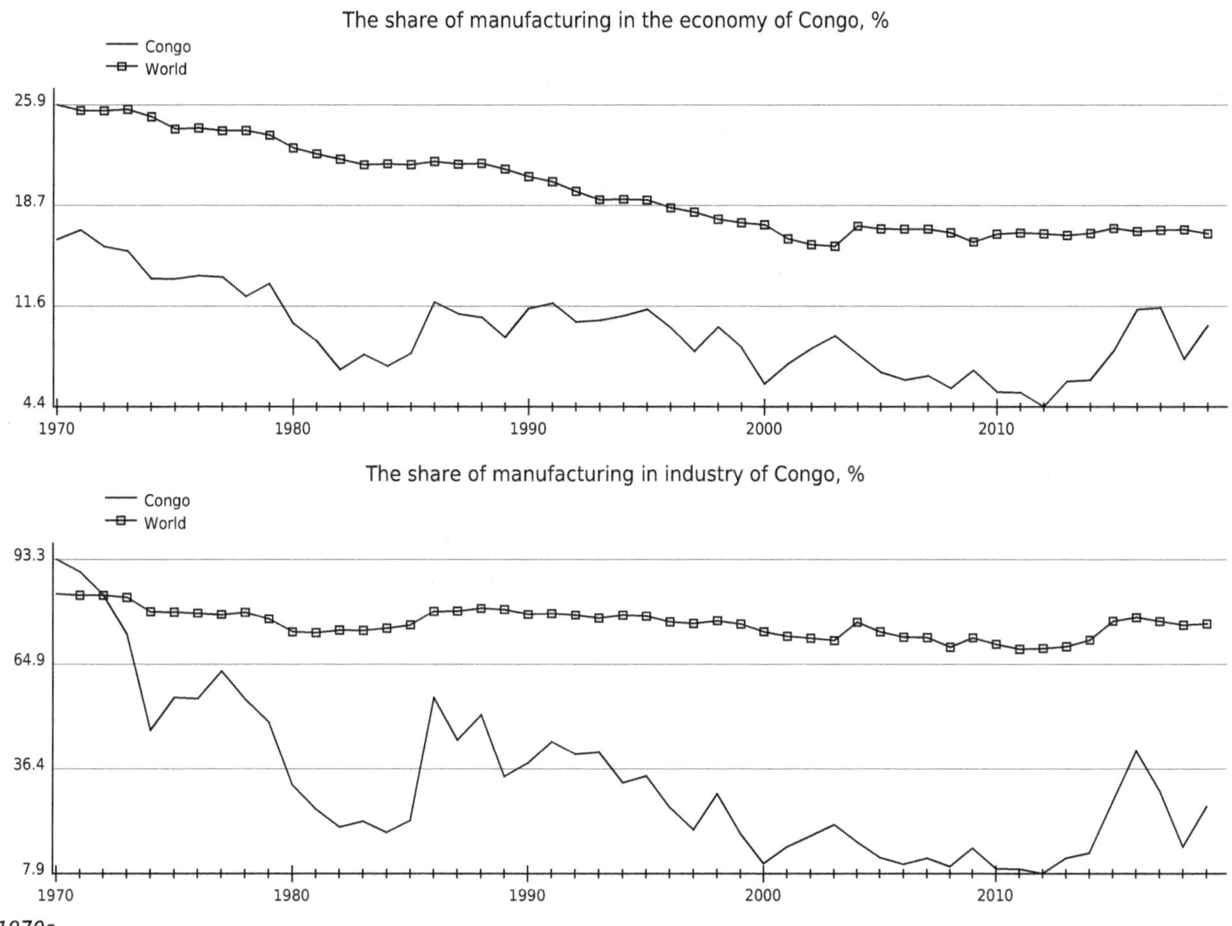

The 1970s

The Congo's manufacturing was $115.1 million per year in the 1970s, ranked 111th in the world. The share in the world was 0.0074%, and 0.28% in Africa.

The share of manufacturing in the economy of Congo was 13.9% in the 1970s, ranked 92nd in the world.

The value of manufacturing per capita in Congo was $75.7 in the 1970s, ranked 105th in the world, and was on a par with Tunisia ($77.2), Nauru ($77.3), Jordan ($74.0). The value added of manufacturing per capita in Congo was less than manufacturing per capita in the world ($383.2) in 5.1 times, and was less than manufacturing per capita in Africa ($99.3) by 23.8%.

The growth of manufacturing in Congo was 0.8% in the 1970s, ranked 164th in the world. The growth of manufacturing in Congo (0.80%) was less than growth of manufacturing in the world (3.8%), was less than growth of manufacturing in Africa (4.9%).

Comparison with neighbors. The sector of manufacturing in Congo was greater than in the CAR ($108.6 million); but less than in DR Congo ($921.8 million), in Angola ($410.3 million), in Cameroon ($376.2 million), and in Gabon ($133.7 million). The manufacturing per capita in Congo was greater than in Angola ($59.4), in the CAR ($55.5), in Cameroon ($50.9), and in DR Congo ($40.6); but less than in Gabon ($207.4). The growth of manufacturing in Congo was greater than in Angola (0.089%) and In DR Congo (-1.4%); but less than in Gabon (8.4%), in Cameroon (6.0%), and in the CAR (3.7%).

Comparison with leaders. The Congo's manufacturing was less than in the USA ($378.0 billion), in the USSR ($248.8 billion), in Japan ($169.3 billion), in Germany ($138.0 billion), and in France ($64.5 billion). The manufacturing per capita in Congo was less than in Germany ($1 752.1), in the USA ($1 731.8), in Japan ($1 520.6), in France ($1 203.0), and in the USSR ($986.6). The growth of manufacturing in Congo was less than in the USSR (5.2%), in Japan (4.5%), in France (3.5%), in the United States (2.7%), and in Germany (2.1%).

The 1980s

The Congo's manufacturing was $249.7 million per year in the 1980s, ranked 113th in the world. The share in the world was 0.0078%, and 0.29% in Africa.

The share of manufacturing in the economy of Congo was 9.4% in the 1980s, ranked 117th in the world.

The value of manufacturing per capita in Congo was $123.1 in the 1980s, ranked 110th in the world, and was on a par with Antigua and Barbuda ($122.5), Côte d'Ivoire ($124.1), Palestine ($124.1). The sector of manufacturing per capita in Congo was less than manufacturing per capita in the world ($661.2) in 5.4 times, and was less than manufacturing per capita in Africa ($157.6) by 21.9%.

The growth of manufacturing in Congo was 7.5% in the 1980s, ranked 29th in the world. The growth of manufacturing in Congo (7.5%) was greater than growth of manufacturing in the world (2.6%), was greater than growth of manufacturing in Africa (2.0%).

Comparison with neighbors. The value added of manufacturing in Congo was greater than in the CAR ($184.2 million); but less than in Cameroon ($1.5 billion), in DR Congo ($1.3 billion), in Angola ($725.3 million), and in Gabon ($265.6 million). The manufacturing per capita in Congo was greater than in the CAR ($73.9), in Angola ($73.8), and in DR Congo ($44.7); but less than in Gabon ($324.0) and in Cameroon ($146.1). The growth of manufacturing in Congo was greater than in Cameroon (6.0%), in DR Congo (2.0%), in Gabon (1.7%), in the Central African Republic (0.53%), and in Angola (-2.4%).

Comparison with leaders. The manufacturing of Congo was less than in the United States ($789.4 billion), in Japan ($501.0 billion), in the USSR ($305.7 billion), in Germany ($258.7 billion), and in Italy ($134.1 billion). The value of manufacturing per capita in Congo was less than in Japan ($4.1 thousand), in Germany ($3.3 thousand), in the USA ($3.3 thousand), in Italy ($2.4 thousand), and in the USSR ($1 110.8). The growth of manufacturing in Congo was greater than in the USSR (5.3%), in Japan (4.4%), in Italy (2.5%), in the United States (1.9%), and in Germany (1.2%).

The 1990s

The Congo's manufacturing was $324.3 million per year in the 1990s, ranked 139th in the world, and was on a par with Kosovo ($325.9 million). The share in the world was 0.0063%, and 0.37% in Africa.

The share of manufacturing in the economy of Congo was 10.4% in the 1990s, ranked 133rd in the world, and was on a par with Namibia (10.5%).

The sector of manufacturing per capita in Congo was $121.0 in the 1990s, ranked 138th in the world, and was on a par with Nicaragua ($120.6), Bosnia and Herzegovina ($122.6), Tajikistan ($119.3). The Congo's manufacturing per capita was less than manufacturing per capita in the world ($908.4) in 7.5 times, and was less than manufacturing per capita in Africa ($124.8) by 3.0%.

The growth of manufacturing in Congo was -3.5% in the 1990s, ranked 175th in the world. The growth of manufacturing in Congo (-3.5%) was less than growth of manufacturing in the world (2.0%), was less than growth of manufacturing in Africa (0.55%).

Comparison with neighbors. The sector of manufacturing in Congo was greater than in Gabon ($268.0 million) and in the CAR ($198.5 million); but less than in Cameroon ($1.7 billion), in DR Congo ($774.3 million), and in Angola ($568.7 million). The manufacturing per capita in Congo was greater than in the CAR ($62.4), in Angola ($41.3), and in DR Congo ($19.1); but less than in Gabon ($249.9) and in Cameroon ($124.7). The growth of manufacturing in Congo was greater than in DR Congo (-10.4%); but less than in Gabon (5.7%), in the Central African Republic (0.68%), in Cameroon (-1.3%), and in Angola (-3.0%).

Comparison with leaders. The Congo's manufacturing was less than in the United States ($1.2 trillion), in Japan ($1.0 trillion), in Germany ($468.8 billion), in Italy ($227.8 billion), and in France ($215.0 billion). The manufacturing per capita in Congo was less than in Japan ($8.3 thousand), in Germany ($5.8 thousand), in the United States ($4.7 thousand), in Italy ($4.0 thousand), and in France ($3.6 thousand). The growth of manufacturing in Congo was less than in the USA (3.2%), in France (2.4%), in Italy (1.2%), in Japan (1.1%), and in Germany (0.26%).

The 2000s

The manufacturing of Congo was $433.3 million per year in the 2000s, ranked 144th in the world. The share in the world was 0.0059%, and 0.33% in Africa.

The share of manufacturing in the economy of Congo was 6.9% in the 2000s, ranked 156th in the world, and was on a par with Saint Kitts and Nevis (6.9%), Greenland (6.9%), Guyana (7.0%).

The value added of manufacturing per capita in Congo was $120.5 in the 2000s, ranked 149th in the world, and was on a par with India ($120.2), Albania ($118.5). The value added of manufacturing per capita in Congo was less than manufacturing per capita in the world ($1 138.1) in 9.4 times, and was less than manufacturing per capita in Africa ($144.8) by 16.8%.

The growth of manufacturing in Congo was 10% in the 2000s, ranked 13th in the world, and was on a par with Belarus (10.0%). The growth of manufacturing in Congo (10.0%) was greater than growth of manufacturing in the world (4.2%), was greater than growth of manufacturing in Africa (3.5%).

Comparison with neighbors. The value of manufacturing in Congo was greater than in Gabon ($401.4 million) and in the CAR ($195.7 million); but less than in Cameroon ($2.6 billion), in DR Congo ($2.1 billion), and in Angola ($1.8 billion). The value added of manufacturing per capita in Congo was greater than in Angola ($92.5), in the Central African Republic ($48.9), and in DR Congo ($39.2); but less than in Gabon ($290.3) and in Cameroon ($147.7). The growth of manufacturing in Congo was greater than in the CAR (5.4%), in Cameroon (4.8%), in Gabon (4.4%), and in DR Congo (-2.9%); but less than in Angola (10.7%).

Comparison with leaders. The value of manufacturing in Congo was less than in the United States ($1.6 trillion), in China ($1.1 trillion), in Japan ($992.9 billion), in Germany ($551.4 billion), and in Italy ($277.2 billion). The sector of manufacturing per capita in Congo was less than in Japan ($7.7 thousand), in Germany ($6.8 thousand), in the United States ($5.6 thousand), in Italy ($4.8 thousand), and in China ($815.3). The growth of manufacturing in Congo was greater than in the United States (1.6%), in Japan (0.32%), in Germany (0.097%), and in Italy (-1.3%).

The 2010s

The value of manufacturing in Congo was $986.1 million per year in the 2010s, ranked 139th in the world, and was on a par with Gabon ($980.5 million), Malta ($974.9 million), Mongolia ($963.4 million). The share in the world was 0.0079%, and 0.41% in Africa.

The share of manufacturing in the economy of Congo was 7.3% in the 2010s, ranked 150th in the world, and was on a par with Australasia (7.3%), Saint Kitts and Nevis (7.3%), Oceania (7.2%).

The sector of manufacturing per capita in Congo was $205.0 in the 2010s, ranked 153rd in the world, and was on a par with Africa ($206.2), Melanesia ($207.8), Cameroon ($208.8). The manufacturing per capita in Congo was less than manufacturing per capita in the world ($1 697.4) in 8.3 times, and was less than manufacturing per capita in Africa ($206.2) by 0.61%.

The growth of manufacturing in Congo was -2.3% in the 2010s, ranked 195th in the world. The growth of manufacturing in Congo (-2.3%) was less than growth of manufacturing in the world (3.9%), was less than growth of manufacturing in Africa (3.6%).

Comparison with neighbors. The value of manufacturing in Congo was 0.57% higher than in Gabon ($980.5 million) and 2.4 times higher than in the Central African Republic ($404.9 million); but 6.5 times lower than in Angola ($6.4 billion), 6.3 times lower than in DR Congo ($6.2 billion), and 4.9 times lower than in Cameroon ($4.8 billion). The value of manufacturing per capita in Congo was 2.3 times higher than in the Central African Republic ($89.6) and 2.5 times higher than in DR Congo ($82.4); but 2.5 times lower than in Gabon ($514.1), 11.6% lower than in Angola ($232.0), and 1.8% lower than in Cameroon ($208.8). The growth of manufacturing in Congo was less than in Gabon (7.3%), in DR Congo (5.3%), in Cameroon (4.5%), in Angola (4.5%), and in the CAR (-1.9%).

Comparison with leaders. The value of manufacturing in Congo was 3 159.0 times lower than in China ($3.1 trillion), 2 099.7 times lower than in the United States ($2.1 trillion), 1 074.9 times lower than in Japan ($1.1 trillion), 745.6 times lower than in Germany ($735.2 billion), and 396.0 times lower than in South Korea ($390.5 billion). The value added of manufacturing per capita in Congo was 43.8 times lower than in Germany ($9.0 thousand), 40.4 times lower than in Japan ($8.3 thousand), 37.7 times lower than in South Korea ($7.7 thousand), 31.6 times lower than in the USA ($6.5 thousand), and 10.8 times lower than in China ($2.2 thousand). The growth of manufacturing in Congo was less than in China (7.5%), in South Korea (3.8%), in Germany (3.5%), in Japan (3.0%), and in the USA (1.9%).

Chapter VI. Construction

(ISIC F)

The value of construction in Congo increased from $19.3 million per year in the 1970s to $1.4 billion per year in the 2010s, that is by $1.4 billion or 72.3 times. The change occurred at $1.1 billion due to a 5.4-fold increase in prices, as also at $196.6 million due to a 4.2-fold increase in productivity, as well as at $41.8 million due to the expansion in population. The average annual growth in construction is 0.93%. The minimum value of construction was in 1970 at $12.3 million. The maximum value of construction was in 2014 at $2.4 billion.

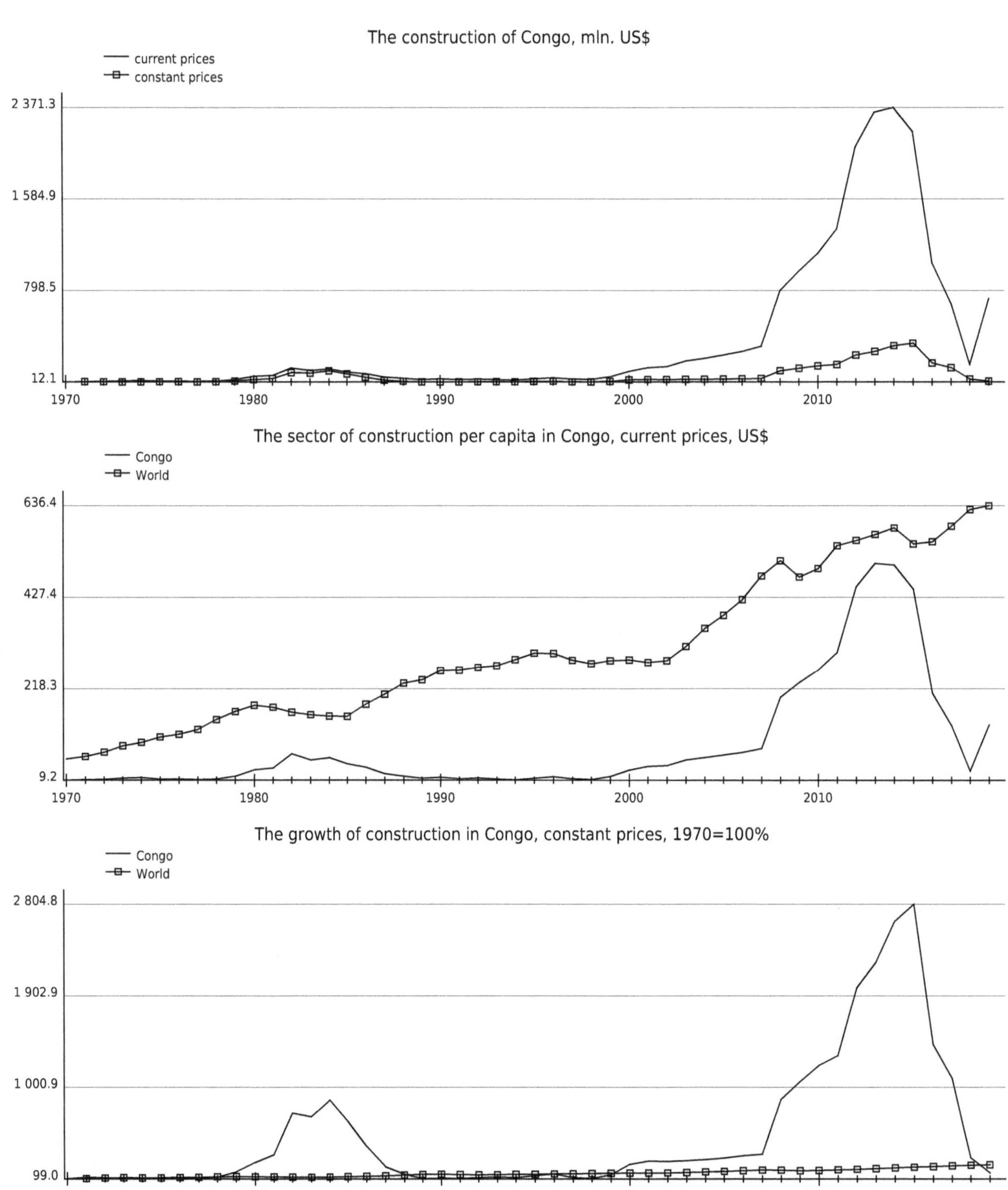

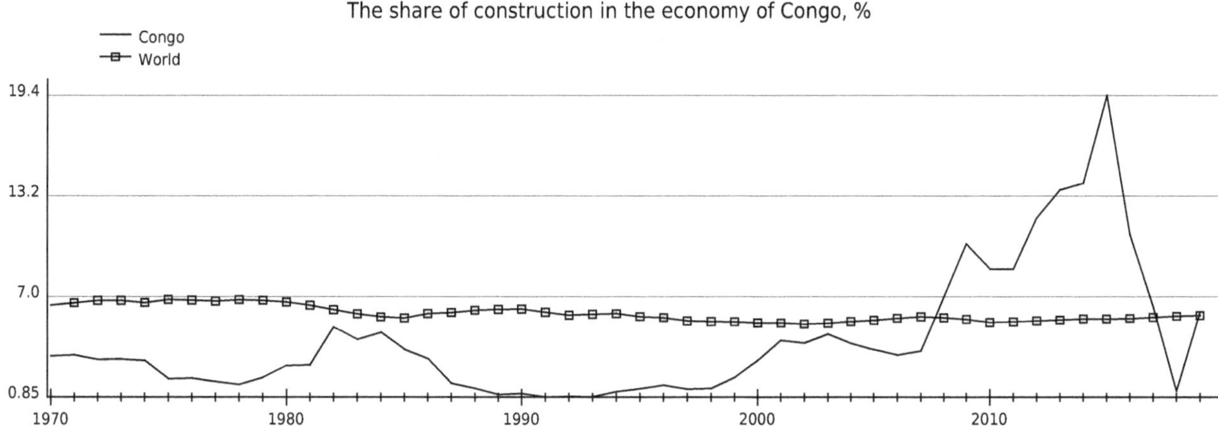

The 1970s

The value added of construction in Congo was $19.3 million per year in the 1970s, ranked 141st in the world, and was on a par with Togo ($19.0 million), Eswatini ($18.9 million), Senegal ($19.8 million). The share in the world was 0.0045%, and 0.12% in Africa.

The share of construction in the economy of Congo was 2.3% in the 1970s, ranked 175th in the world.

The construction per capita in Congo was $12.7 in the 1970s, ranked 148th in the world, and was on a par with the Maldives ($12.5). The value of construction per capita in Congo was less than construction per capita in the world ($106.1) in 8.4 times, and was less than construction per capita in Africa ($39.9) in 3.1 times.

The growth of construction in Congo was 5.7% in the 1970s, ranked 75th in the world, and was on a par with Cameroon (5.7%). The growth of construction in Congo (5.7%) was greater than growth of construction in the world (2.1%), was greater than growth of construction in Africa (4.5%).

Comparison with neighbors. The construction of Congo was greater than in the Central African Republic ($4.3 million); but less than in DR Congo ($405.2 million), in Cameroon ($271.5 million), in Angola ($209.1 million), and in Gabon ($190.2 million). The value of construction per capita in Congo was greater than in the CAR ($2.2); but less than in Gabon ($295.0), in Cameroon ($36.7), in Angola ($30.3), and in DR Congo ($17.9). The growth of construction in Congo was greater than in Cameroon (5.7%), in the Central African Republic (1.5%), in Angola (0.15%), and in DR Congo (-1.3%); but less than in Gabon (8.1%).

Comparison with leaders. The Congo's construction was less than in the USA ($81.1 billion), in the USSR ($52.5 billion), in Japan ($43.5 billion), in Germany ($33.8 billion), and in France ($22.4 billion). The value of construction per capita in Congo was less than in Germany ($428.6), in France ($417.3), in Japan ($390.8), in the USA ($371.5), and in the USSR ($208.1). The growth of construction in Congo was greater than in Japan (3.4%), in France (2.0%), in Germany (0.66%), and in the USA (0.31%); but less than in the USSR (6.5%).

The 1980s

The Congo's construction was $80.1 million per year in the 1980s, ranked 121st in the world, and was on a par with Rwanda ($80.1 million), Burkina Faso ($80.9 million), Bermuda ($78.4 million). The share in the world was 0.0089%, and 0.28% in Africa.

The share of construction in the economy of Congo was 3.0% in the 1980s, ranked 160th in the world, and was on a par with Madagascar (3.0%), Pakistan (3.0%), El Salvador (3.0%).

The construction per capita in Congo was $39.4 in the 1980s, ranked 128th in the world, and was on a par with Peru ($39.4), Angola ($38.8). The Congo's construction per capita was less than construction per capita in the world ($186.2) in 4.7 times, and was less than construction per capita in Africa ($53.3) by 25.9%.

The growth of construction in Congo was -4.9% in the 1980s, ranked 168th in the world. The growth of construction in Congo (-4.9%) was less than growth of construction in the world (1.7%), was less than growth of construction in Africa (0.41%).

Comparison with neighbors. The sector of construction in Congo was greater than in the Central African Republic ($9.8 million); but less than in Cameroon ($870.6 million), in DR Congo ($464.3 million), in Angola ($381.0 million), and in Gabon ($196.1 million). The value of construction per capita in Congo was greater than in Angola ($38.8), in DR Congo ($15.7), and in the Central African

Republic ($3.9); but less than in Gabon ($239.2) and in Cameroon ($87.4). The growth of construction in Congo was less than in the CAR (8.4%), in Gabon (1.9%), in Angola (1.2%), in DR Congo (0.82%), and in Cameroon (-4.0%).

Comparison with leaders. The Congo's construction was less than in the United States ($180.6 billion), in Japan ($138.7 billion), in the USSR ($72.1 billion), in Germany ($57.8 billion), and in France ($42.5 billion). The sector of construction per capita in Congo was less than in Japan ($1 143.9), in the United States ($754.4), in France ($751.9), in Germany ($740.2), and in the USSR ($262.0). The growth of construction in Congo was less than in the USSR (6.2%), in Japan (2.1%), in the USA (1.1%), in France (0.67%), and in Germany (-0.52%).

The 1990s

The value added of construction in Congo was $37.9 million per year in the 1990s, ranked 176th in the world. The share in the world was 0.0024%, and 0.15% in Africa.

The share of construction in the economy of Congo was 1.2% in the 1990s, ranked 208th in the world.

The sector of construction per capita in Congo was $14.1 in the 1990s, ranked 181st in the world, and was on a par with Tajikistan ($13.9). The value of construction per capita in Congo was less than construction per capita in the world ($278.6) in 19.7 times, and was less than construction per capita in Africa ($34.6) in 2.4 times.

The growth of construction in Congo was 3.3% in the 1990s, ranked 97th in the world, and was on a par with Malawi (3.3%). The growth of construction in Congo (3.3%) was greater than growth of construction in the world (0.71%), was greater than growth of construction in Africa (2.8%).

Comparison with neighbors. The construction of Congo was greater than in the CAR ($22.2 million); but less than in Cameroon ($621.6 million), in Angola ($464.5 million), in DR Congo ($391.9 million), and in Gabon ($195.4 million). The value of construction per capita in Congo was greater than in DR Congo ($9.7) and in the Central African Republic ($7.0); but less than in Gabon ($182.3), in Cameroon ($46.3), and in Angola ($33.7). The growth of construction in Congo was greater than in Angola (3.0%), in Gabon (1.9%), in Cameroon (-2.8%), in the CAR (-4.4%), and in DR Congo (-15.1%).

Comparison with leaders. The construction of Congo was less than in Japan ($343.2 billion), in the USA ($299.1 billion), in Germany ($125.2 billion), in the UK ($69.8 billion), and in France ($68.8 billion). The value added of construction per capita in Congo was less than in Japan ($2.7 thousand), in Germany ($1 552.3), in the UK ($1 205.1), in France ($1 158.8), and in the USA ($1 131.2). The growth of construction in Congo was greater than in the USA (1.8%), in Germany (-0.047%), in the UK (-0.34%), in France (-0.65%), and in Japan (-1.0%).

The 2000s

The sector of construction in Congo was $338.1 million per year in the 2000s, ranked 130th in the world, and was on a par with Malta ($338.3 million). The share in the world was 0.014%, and 0.69% in Africa.

The share of construction in the economy of Congo was 5.4% in the 2000s, ranked 123rd in the world, and was on a par with Rwanda (5.4%), Nicaragua (5.4%), Guatemala (5.4%).

The sector of construction per capita in Congo was $94.0 in the 2000s, ranked 137th in the world. The sector of construction per capita in Congo was less than construction per capita in the world ($381.3) in 4.1 times, and was greater than construction per capita in Africa ($53.8) by 74.9%.

The growth of construction in Congo was 22.5% in the 2000s, ranked 4th in the world. The growth of construction in Congo (22.5%) was greater than growth of construction in the world (1.5%), was greater than growth of construction in Africa (8.4%).

Comparison with neighbors. The Congo's construction was greater than in Gabon ($247.0 million) and in the CAR ($29.6 million); but less than in Angola ($2.7 billion), in Cameroon ($851.1 million), and in DR Congo ($475.6 million). The value added of construction per capita in Congo was greater than in Cameroon ($48.5), in DR Congo ($8.8), and in the CAR ($7.4); but less than in Gabon ($178.6) and in Angola ($141.8). The growth of construction in Congo was greater than in DR Congo (19.4%), in Cameroon (18.8%), in Angola (11.2%), in Gabon (5.2%), and in the Central African Republic (4.4%).

Comparison with leaders. The sector of construction in Congo was less than in the USA ($583.0 billion), in Japan ($270.5 billion), in China ($150.1 billion), in the UK ($132.1 billion), and in Spain ($111.8 billion). The value added of construction per capita in Congo was less than in Spain ($2.6 thousand), in the UK ($2.2 thousand), in Japan ($2.1 thousand), in the USA ($1 983.7), and in China ($113.1). The growth of construction in Congo was greater than in China (11.9%), in Spain (1.7%), in the UK (0.17%), in the United States (-2.6%), and in Japan (-3.9%).

The 2010s

The construction of Congo was $1.4 billion per year in the 2010s, ranked 105th in the world, and was on a par with North Korea ($1.4 billion), Trinidad and Tobago ($1.4 billion), Nepal ($1.4 billion). The share in the world was 0.033%, and 1.1% in Africa.

The share of construction in the economy of Congo was 10.3% in the 2010s, ranked 22nd in the world, and was on a par with Uruguay (10.3%), Indonesia (10.3%), Turkmenistan (10.4%).

The sector of construction per capita in Congo was $289.8 in the 2010s, ranked 123rd in the world, and was on a par with Central Asia ($288.8), Kosovo ($287.1). The construction per capita in Congo was less than construction per capita in the world ($572.1) by 49.3%, and was greater than construction per capita in Africa ($109.4) in 2.6 times.

The growth of construction in Congo was -17.3% in the 2010s, ranked 209th in the world. The growth of construction in Congo (-17.3%) was less than growth of construction in the world (2.9%), was less than growth of construction in Africa (5.8%).

Comparison with neighbors. The value of construction in Congo was 57.8% higher than in Gabon ($883.9 million), 3.7 times higher than in DR Congo ($376.2 million), and 33.3 times higher than in the CAR ($41.9 million); but 9.5 times lower than in Angola ($13.2 billion) and 12.1% lower than in Cameroon ($1.6 billion). The construction per capita in Congo was 4.2 times higher than in Cameroon ($68.9), 31.3 times higher than in the Central African Republic ($9.3), and 58.0 times higher than in DR Congo ($5.0); but 39.6% lower than in Angola ($479.9) and 37.5% lower than in Gabon ($463.5). The growth of construction in Congo was greater than in the Central African Republic (-17.6%); but less than in DR Congo (8.9%), in Cameroon (6.5%), in Angola (5.9%), and in Gabon (3.4%).

Comparison with leaders. The Congo's construction was 524.3 times lower than in China ($731.1 billion), 488.2 times lower than in the USA ($680.8 billion), 199.8 times lower than in Japan ($278.7 billion), 120.5 times lower than in India ($168.1 billion), and 109.9 times lower than in Germany ($153.2 billion). The sector of construction per capita in Congo was 2.2 times higher than in India ($129.1); but 7.5 times lower than in Japan ($2.2 thousand), 7.4 times lower than in the USA ($2.1 thousand), 6.5 times lower than in Germany ($1 871.9), and 44.4% lower than in China ($521.3). The growth of construction in Congo was less than in China (8.2%), in India (5.2%), in Germany (1.8%), in Japan (1.7%), and in the United States (1.4%).

Chapter VII. Transportation

Transport, storage and communication (ISIC I)

The value of transportation in Congo rose from $111.9 million per year in the 1970s to $941.6 million per year in the 2010s, that is by $829.7 million or 8.4 times. The change occurred at $453.6 million due to a 1.9-fold increase in prices, as also at $133.8 million due to a 1.4-fold increase in productivity, as well as at $242.4 million due to the rise in population. The average annual growth in transportation is 3.1%. The minimum value of transportation was in 1970 at $54.5 million. The maximum value of transportation was in 2013 at $1.2 billion.

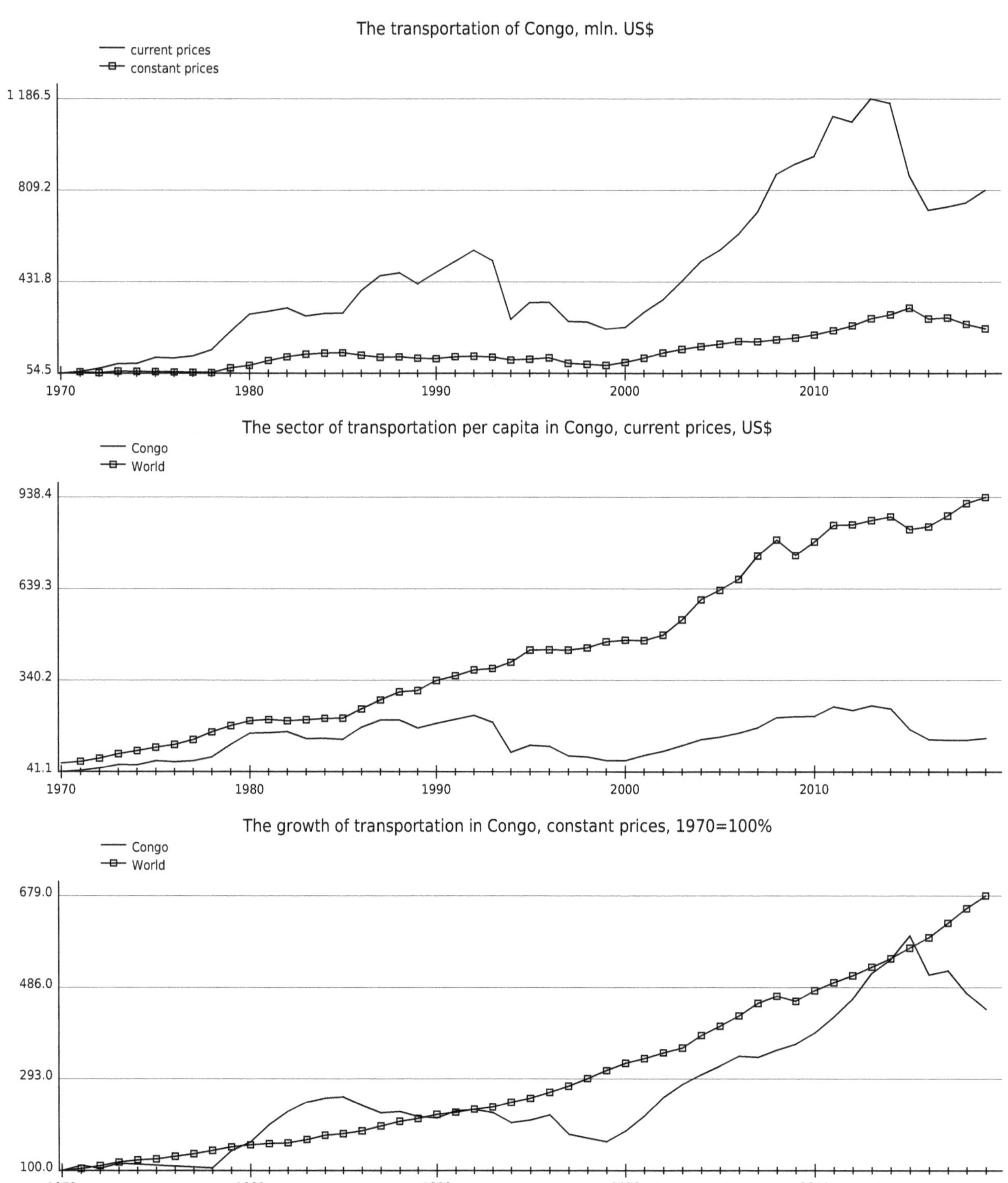

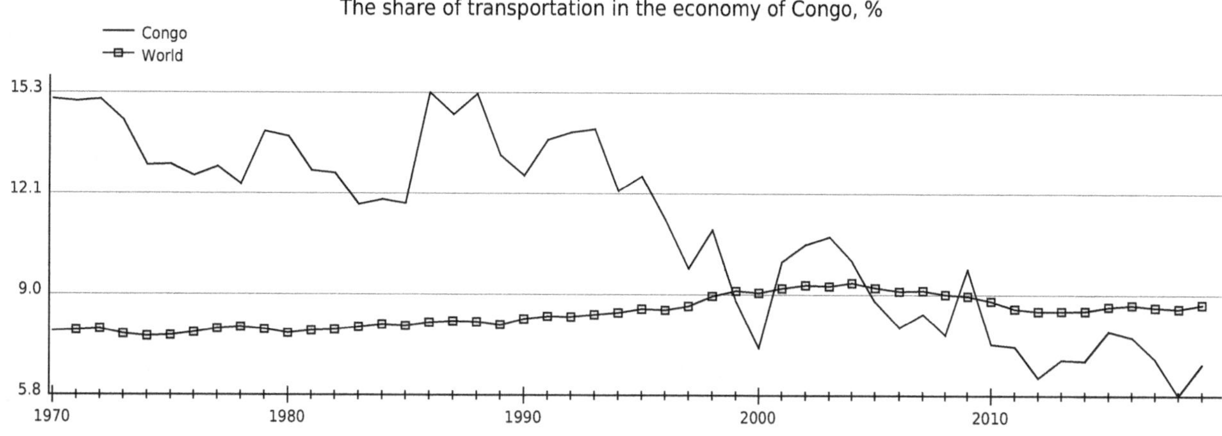

The 1970s

The Congo's transportation was $111.9 million per year in the 1970s, ranked 97th in the world, and was on a par with Vietnam ($111.6 million), Paraguay ($110.1 million), Afghanistan ($114.0 million). The share in the world was 0.023%, and 0.49% in Africa.

The share of transportation in the economy of Congo was 13.5% in the 1970s, ranked 5th in the world.

The sector of transportation per capita in Congo was $73.6 in the 1970s, ranked 79th in the world. The sector of transportation per capita in Congo was less than transportation per capita in the world ($122.3) by 39.8%, and was greater than transportation per capita in Africa ($55.9) by 31.8%.

The growth of transportation in Congo was 3.9% in the 1970s, ranked 123rd in the world. The growth of transportation in Congo (3.9%) was less than growth of transportation in the world (4.6%), was less than growth of transportation in Africa (6.8%).

Comparison with neighbors. The value of transportation in Congo was greater than in Gabon ($90.7 million) and in the Central African Republic ($7.2 million); but less than in DR Congo ($899.5 million), in Cameroon ($284.8 million), and in Angola ($197.8 million). The value of transportation per capita in Congo was greater than in DR Congo ($39.6), in Cameroon ($38.5), in Angola ($28.6), and in the Central African Republic ($3.7); but less than in Gabon ($140.8). The growth of transportation in Congo was greater than in Angola (0.064%), in DR Congo (-0.33%), and in the Central African Republic (-0.35%); but less than in Gabon (8.3%) and in Cameroon (5.7%).

Comparison with leaders. The Congo's transportation was less than in the United States ($168.6 billion), in Japan ($46.4 billion), in Germany ($29.6 billion), in the USSR ($28.8 billion), and in France ($24.0 billion). The sector of transportation per capita in Congo was less than in the United States ($772.4), in France ($447.4), in Japan ($416.6), in Germany ($376.1), and in the USSR ($114.0). The growth of transportation in Congo was greater than in Germany (3.0%) and in Japan (1.7%); but less than in the USSR (8.1%), in the United States (4.2%), and in France (4.1%).

The 1980s

The value added of transportation in Congo was $357.4 million per year in the 1980s, ranked 88th in the world, and was on a par with Guatemala ($359.0 million), Angola ($351.0 million). The share in the world was 0.031%, and 0.73% in Africa.

The share of transportation in the economy of Congo was 13.4% in the 1980s, ranked 10th in the world, and was on a par with Sierra Leone (13.4%).

The value of transportation per capita in Congo was $176.1 in the 1980s, ranked 73rd in the world, and was on a par with Grenada ($176.7), Central America ($174.2). The value of transportation per capita in Congo was less than transportation per capita in the world ($242.0) by 27.2%, and was greater than transportation per capita in Africa ($90.3) by 95.0%.

The growth of transportation in Congo was 4.2% in the 1980s, ranked 78th in the world, and was on a par with Oceania (4.2%), Swaziland (4.2%), Turkey (4.2%). The growth of transportation in Congo (4.2%) was greater than growth of transportation in the world (3.4%), was greater than growth of transportation in Africa (-0.23%).

Comparison with neighbors. The value of transportation in Congo was greater than in Angola ($351.0 million), in Gabon ($276.1 million), and in the Central African Republic ($15.7 million); but less than in DR Congo ($1.6 billion) and in Cameroon ($701.6 million).

The value of transportation per capita in Congo was greater than in Cameroon ($70.5), in DR Congo ($53.0), in Angola ($35.7), and in the CAR ($6.3); but less than in Gabon ($336.8). The growth of transportation in Congo was greater than in the CAR (3.2%), in Angola (2.3%), in Cameroon (1.9%), in DR Congo (1.8%), and in Gabon (1.3%).

Comparison with leaders. The Congo's transportation was less than in the United States ($394.9 billion), in Japan ($147.7 billion), in Germany ($56.6 billion), in France ($56.2 billion), and in the UK ($53.0 billion). The transportation per capita in Congo was less than in the United States ($1 649.2), in Japan ($1 217.8), in France ($993.7), in the UK ($938.7), and in Germany ($725.5). The growth of transportation in Congo was greater than in the USA (3.6%), in the United Kingdom (3.0%), and in Germany (1.8%); but less than in France (5.4%) and in Japan (4.7%).

The 1990s

The sector of transportation in Congo was $380.9 million per year in the 1990s, ranked 108th in the world. The share in the world was 0.016%, and 0.85% in Africa.

The share of transportation in the economy of Congo was 12.3% in the 1990s, ranked 21st in the world, and was on a par with Eritrea (12.2%), Montserrat (12.2%).

The transportation per capita in Congo was $142.1 in the 1990s, ranked 106th in the world, and was on a par with Ecuador ($142.3). The transportation per capita in Congo was less than transportation per capita in the world ($409.5) in 2.9 times, and was greater than transportation per capita in Africa ($63.1) in 2.3 times.

The growth of transportation in Congo was -2.8% in the 1990s, ranked 185th in the world. The growth of transportation in Congo (-2.8%) was less than growth of transportation in the world (4.0%), was less than growth of transportation in Africa (3.3%).

Comparison with neighbors. The transportation of Congo was greater than in Angola ($295.8 million) and in the Central African Republic ($22.2 million); but less than in DR Congo ($1.4 billion), in Cameroon ($879.5 million), and in Gabon ($403.7 million). The value added of transportation per capita in Congo was greater than in Cameroon ($65.5), in DR Congo ($35.3), in Angola ($21.5), and in the CAR ($7.0); but less than in Gabon ($376.5). The growth of transportation in Congo was less than in the Central African Republic (7.6%), in Gabon (2.3%), in Cameroon (1.3%), in Angola (-1.6%), and in DR Congo (-1.9%).

Comparison with leaders. The value of transportation in Congo was less than in the USA ($702.6 billion), in Japan ($373.9 billion), in Germany ($144.3 billion), in France ($118.7 billion), and in the UK ($117.6 billion). The transportation per capita in Congo was less than in Japan ($3.0 thousand), in the USA ($2.7 thousand), in the UK ($2.0 thousand), in France ($1 999.2), and in Germany ($1 789.0). The growth of transportation in Congo was less than in the United States (5.0%), in France (4.8%), in the United Kingdom (4.7%), in Germany (3.9%), and in Japan (3.0%).

The 2000s

The transportation of Congo was $556.0 million per year in the 2000s, ranked 123rd in the world, and was on a par with Ethiopia ($546.1 million), Polynesia ($566.2 million), Haiti ($570.1 million). The share in the world was 0.014%, and 0.62% in Africa.

The share of transportation in the economy of Congo was 8.9% in the 2000s, ranked 109th in the world, and was on a par with Curaçao (8.9%), Uruguay (8.8%), Eastern Africa (8.8%).

The value of transportation per capita in Congo was $154.6 in the 2000s, ranked 135th in the world, and was on a par with the FSM ($155.0), Sri Lanka ($151.3). The Congo's transportation per capita was less than transportation per capita in the world ($621.1) in 4.0 times, and was greater than transportation per capita in Africa ($99.3) by 55.6%.

The growth of transportation in Congo was 8.6% in the 2000s, ranked 51st in the world, and was on a par with Venezuela (8.5%), Southern Asia (8.5%), Morocco (8.6%). The growth of transportation in Congo (8.6%) was greater than growth of transportation in the world (3.9%), was greater than growth of transportation in Africa (7.8%).

Comparison with neighbors. The transportation of Congo was greater than in Gabon ($467.0 million) and in the Central African Republic ($36.2 million); but less than in DR Congo ($1.7 billion), in Angola ($1.4 billion), and in Cameroon ($1.4 billion). The sector of transportation per capita in Congo was greater than in Cameroon ($79.2), in Angola ($74.3), in DR Congo ($31.5), and in the CAR ($9.1); but less than in Gabon ($337.7). The growth of transportation in Congo was greater than in Angola (8.3%), in DR Congo (6.2%), in Cameroon (4.7%), in Gabon (3.1%), and in the Central African Republic (0.99%).

Comparison with leaders. The transportation of Congo was less than in the United States ($1.2 trillion), in Japan ($468.5 billion), in Germany ($228.2 billion), in the UK ($215.9 billion), and in France ($185.6 billion). The value added of transportation per capita in Congo was less than in the United States ($4.0 thousand), in Japan ($3.7 thousand), in the UK ($3.6 thousand), in France ($3.0 thousand), and in Germany ($2.8 thousand). The growth of transportation in Congo was greater than in Germany (3.4%), in the UK (3.1%), in the United States (3.1%), in France (2.7%), and in Japan (1.5%).

The 2010s

The value of transportation in Congo was $941.6 million per year in the 2010s, ranked 126th in the world, and was on a par with Tajikistan ($962.0 million), the Bahamas ($919.0 million). The share in the world was 0.015%, and 0.46% in Africa.

The share of transportation in the economy of Congo was 7.0% in the 2010s, ranked 156th in the world, and was on a par with Armenia (7.0%), Gambia (7.0%), Honduras (7.0%).

The Congo's transportation per capita was $195.7 in the 2010s, ranked 148th in the world, and was on a par with São Tomé and Príncipe ($191.0). The sector of transportation per capita in Congo was less than transportation per capita in the world ($864.8) in 4.4 times, and was greater than transportation per capita in Africa ($173.7) by 12.7%.

The growth of transportation in Congo was 1.8% in the 2010s, ranked 169th in the world, and was on a par with Greenland (1.8%). The growth of transportation in Congo (1.8%) was less than growth of transportation in the world (4.0%), was less than growth of transportation in Africa (3.8%).

Comparison with neighbors. The sector of transportation in Congo was 4.2% higher than in Gabon ($903.8 million) and 19.8 times higher than in the CAR ($47.5 million); but 5.5 times lower than in Angola ($5.1 billion), 3.5 times lower than in DR Congo ($3.3 billion), and 2.7 times lower than in Cameroon ($2.5 billion). The value added of transportation per capita in Congo was 4.8% higher than in Angola ($186.8), 77.5% higher than in Cameroon ($110.2), 4.4 times higher than in DR Congo ($44.3), and 18.6 times higher than in the Central African Republic ($10.5); but 2.4 times lower than in Gabon ($473.9). The growth of transportation in Congo was less than in the Central African Republic (9.4%), in Gabon (7.9%), in Angola (7.1%), in Cameroon (4.8%), and in DR Congo (3.5%).

Comparison with leaders. The Congo's transportation was 1 899.3 times lower than in the USA ($1.8 trillion), 562.7 times lower than in Japan ($529.8 billion), 493.0 times lower than in China ($464.2 billion), 318.6 times lower than in Germany ($300.0 billion), and 273.7 times lower than in the UK ($257.7 billion). The value added of transportation per capita in Congo was 28.6 times lower than in the USA ($5.6 thousand), 21.2 times lower than in Japan ($4.1 thousand), 20.1 times lower than in the United Kingdom ($3.9 thousand), 18.7 times lower than in Germany ($3.7 thousand), and 40.9% lower than in China ($331.0). The growth of transportation in Congo was greater than in Japan (0.81%); but less than in China (7.5%), in the USA (5.1%), in the UK (2.8%), and in Germany (2.7%).

Chapter VIII. Trade

Wholesale, retail trade, restaurants and hotels (ISIC G-H)

The value of trade in Congo increased from $109.0 million per year in the 1970s to $1.5 billion per year in the 2010s, that is by $1.4 billion or 13.6 times. The change occurred at $995.4 million due to a 3.0-fold increase in prices, as also at $144.7 million due to a 1.4-fold increase in productivity, as well as at $236.1 million due to the growth in population. The average annual growth in trade is 3.3%. The minimum value of trade was in 1970 at $43.8 million. The maximum value of trade was in 2018 at $1.8 billion.

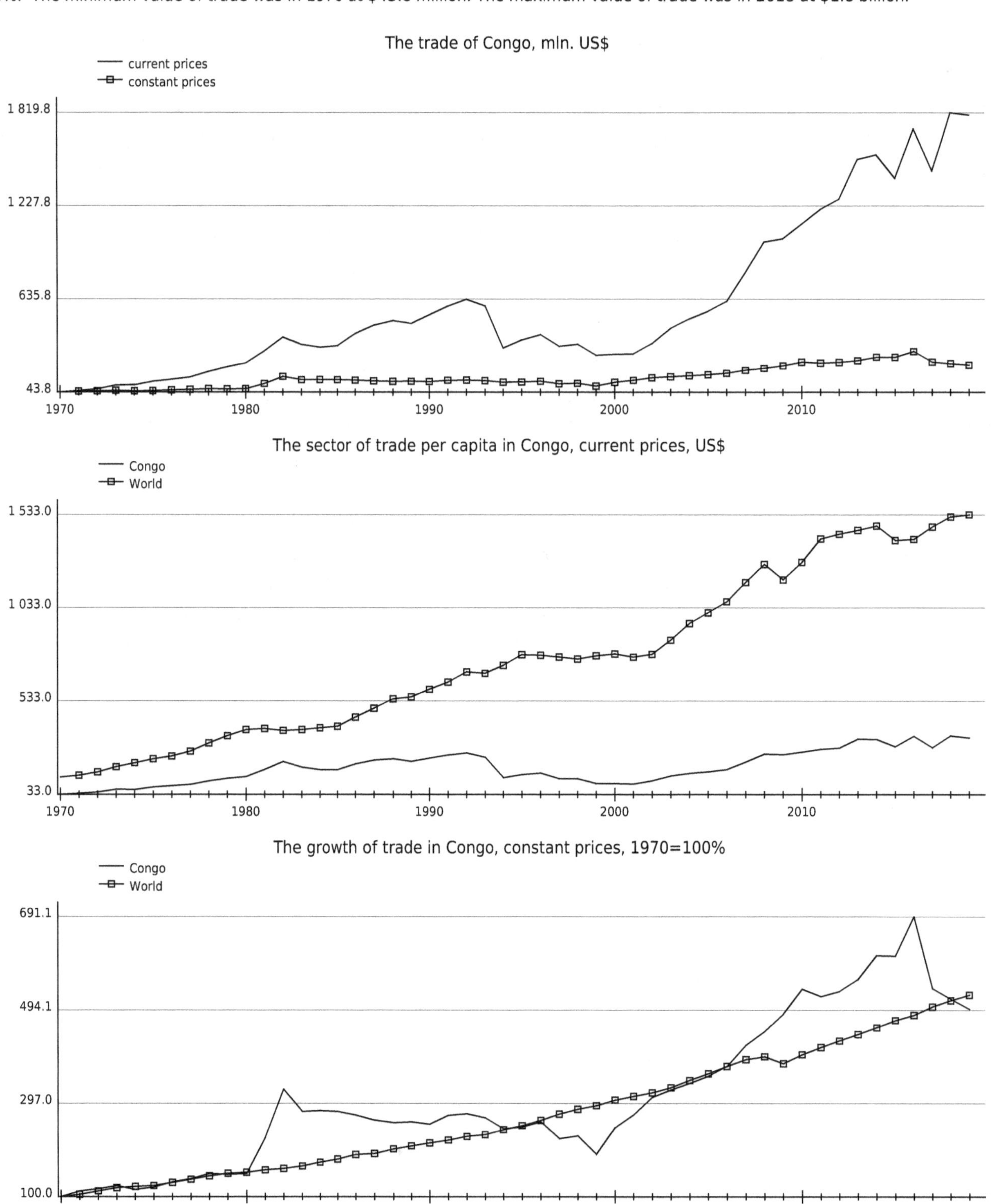

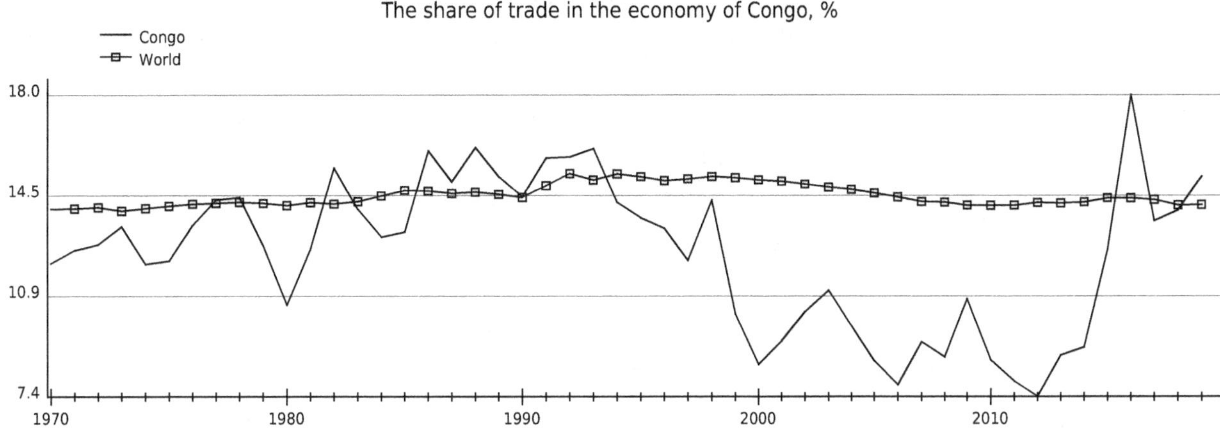

The 1970s

The sector of trade in Congo was $109.0 million per year in the 1970s, ranked 120th in the world, and was on a par with Guyana ($109.8 million), Polynesia ($111.7 million). The share in the world was 0.012%, and 0.36% in Africa.

The share of trade in the economy of Congo was 13.1% in the 1970s, ranked 115th in the world, and was on a par with Tonga (13.1%), the FSM (13.2%), Tunisia (13.1%).

The trade per capita in Congo was $71.7 in the 1970s, ranked 127th in the world, and was on a par with Middle Africa ($71.7), Saint Kitts and Nevis ($70.8). The Congo's trade per capita was less than trade per capita in the world ($221.0) in 3.1 times, and was less than trade per capita in Africa ($73.8) by 2.8%.

The growth of trade in Congo was 4.4% in the 1970s, ranked 103rd in the world. The growth of trade in Congo (4.4%) was less than growth of trade in the world (4.5%), was less than growth of trade in Africa (4.6%).

Comparison with neighbors. The value added of trade in Congo was greater than in the CAR ($82.1 million); but less than in DR Congo ($1.6 billion), in Angola ($564.8 million), in Cameroon ($549.0 million), and in Gabon ($137.4 million). The sector of trade per capita in Congo was greater than in DR Congo ($69.7) and in the Central African Republic ($42.0); but less than in Gabon ($213.2), in Angola ($81.7), and in Cameroon ($74.3). The growth of trade in Congo was greater than in DR Congo (3.6%), in Angola (0.17%), and in the CAR (-1.2%); but less than in Gabon (8.3%) and in Cameroon (5.7%).

Comparison with leaders. The value of trade in Congo was less than in the USA ($278.3 billion), in Japan ($90.3 billion), in the USSR ($62.3 billion), in Germany ($61.1 billion), and in France ($40.9 billion). The trade per capita in Congo was less than in the USA ($1 275.1), in Japan ($811.1), in Germany ($775.5), in France ($762.4), and in the USSR ($247.1). The growth of trade in Congo was greater than in France (3.9%), in the United States (3.9%), and in Germany (3.0%); but less than in Japan (8.2%) and in the USSR (5.2%).

The 1980s

The trade of Congo was $380.7 million per year in the 1980s, ranked 112th in the world. The share in the world was 0.018%, and 0.58% in Africa.

The share of trade in the economy of Congo was 14.3% in the 1980s, ranked 100th in the world, and was on a par with Jordan (14.2%), Laos (14.3%), Eastern Asia (14.4%).

The trade per capita in Congo was $187.6 in the 1980s, ranked 103rd in the world, and was on a par with Guinea ($186.9), Vanuatu ($184.8). The value of trade per capita in Congo was less than trade per capita in the world ($437.7) in 2.3 times, and was greater than trade per capita in Africa ($121.8) by 54.0%.

The growth of trade in Congo was 5.8% in the 1980s, ranked 28th in the world, and was on a par with Asia (5.8%), South-Eastern Asia (5.8%). The growth of trade in Congo (5.8%) was greater than growth of trade in the world (3.3%), was greater than growth of trade in Africa (2.7%).

Comparison with neighbors. The trade of Congo was greater than in Gabon ($313.4 million) and in the Central African Republic ($172.1 million); but less than in DR Congo ($1.6 billion), in Cameroon ($1.4 billion), and in Angola ($1.0 billion). The sector of trade per capita in Congo was greater than in Cameroon ($144.8), in Angola ($106.1), in the Central African Republic ($69.1), and in DR Congo ($54.8); but less than in Gabon ($382.3). The growth of trade in Congo was greater than in Angola (3.4%), in Cameroon (1.9%), in DR Congo (1.8%), in Gabon (1.2%), and in the CAR (0.20%).

Comparison with leaders. The trade of Congo was less than in the United States ($653.3 billion), in Japan ($277.3 billion), in Germany ($116.7 billion), in the USSR ($112.3 billion), and in Italy ($95.7 billion). The value added of trade per capita in Congo was less than in the USA ($2.7 thousand), in Japan ($2.3 thousand), in Italy ($1 684.2), in Germany ($1 496.0), and in the USSR ($408.1). The growth of trade in Congo was greater than in Japan (4.9%), in the USA (4.4%), in Italy (2.3%), in Germany (1.8%), and in the USSR (-0.62%).

The 1990s

The value of trade in Congo was $442.3 million per year in the 1990s, ranked 135th in the world, and was on a par with Burkina Faso ($443.0 million), Cambodia ($444.7 million), Aruba ($446.5 million). The share in the world was 0.011%, and 0.52% in Africa.

The share of trade in the economy of Congo was 14.2% in the 1990s, ranked 112th in the world, and was on a par with Uganda (14.2%), the United Kingdom (14.2%), Palestine (14.2%).

The trade per capita in Congo was $165.0 in the 1990s, ranked 132nd in the world, and was on a par with Kosovo ($166.7), Morocco ($168.4). The value of trade per capita in Congo was less than trade per capita in the world ($721.8) in 4.4 times, and was greater than trade per capita in Africa ($120.3) by 37.1%.

The growth of trade in Congo was -3.1% in the 1990s, ranked 188th in the world, and was on a par with Kazakhstan (-3.0%). The growth of trade in Congo (-3.1%) was less than growth of trade in the world (3.5%), was less than growth of trade in Africa (2.8%).

Comparison with neighbors. The Congo's trade was greater than in the CAR ($165.9 million); but less than in Cameroon ($1.6 billion), in DR Congo ($1.5 billion), in Angola ($1.1 billion), and in Gabon ($458.6 million). The value added of trade per capita in Congo was greater than in Cameroon ($119.0), in Angola ($83.2), in the CAR ($52.2), and in DR Congo ($36.6); but less than in Gabon ($427.7). The growth of trade in Congo was less than in Cameroon (1.4%), in Gabon (0.75%), in the CAR (-1.8%), in DR Congo (-2.3%), and in Angola (-2.4%).

Comparison with leaders. The value added of trade in Congo was less than in the USA ($1.2 trillion), in Japan ($713.2 billion), in Germany ($243.7 billion), in Italy ($185.6 billion), and in France ($177.0 billion). The trade per capita in Congo was less than in Japan ($5.7 thousand), in the United States ($4.4 thousand), in Italy ($3.3 thousand), in Germany ($3.0 thousand), and in France ($3.0 thousand). The growth of trade in Congo was less than in the United States (4.3%), in Japan (3.8%), in Germany (2.5%), in France (2.4%), and in Italy (1.9%).

The 2000s

The value added of trade in Congo was $588.8 million per year in the 2000s, ranked 144th in the world, and was on a par with Afghanistan ($584.8 million), Benin ($594.8 million). The share in the world was 0.0091%, and 0.40% in Africa.

The share of trade in the economy of Congo was 9.4% in the 2000s, ranked 189th in the world, and was on a par with Sierra Leone (9.4%), Afghanistan (9.4%), Norway (9.5%).

The trade per capita in Congo was $163.7 in the 2000s, ranked 154th in the world, and was on a par with Africa ($164.0), Djibouti ($162.7), Zambia ($165.8). The value of trade per capita in Congo was less than trade per capita in the world ($990.3) in 6.1 times, and was less than trade per capita in Africa ($164.0) by 0.18%.

The growth of trade in Congo was 9.9% in the 2000s, ranked 22nd in the world, and was on a par with Uzbekistan (9.9%), Montenegro (10.0%). The growth of trade in Congo (9.9%) was greater than growth of trade in the world (2.7%), was greater than growth of trade in Africa (5.9%).

Comparison with neighbors. The Congo's trade was greater than in Gabon ($509.8 million) and in the Central African Republic ($188.2 million); but less than in Angola ($5.2 billion), in Cameroon ($3.1 billion), and in DR Congo ($1.6 billion). The value added of trade per capita in Congo was greater than in the CAR ($47.1) and in DR Congo ($30.4); but less than in Gabon ($368.6), in Angola ($270.3), and in Cameroon ($174.2). The growth of trade in Congo was greater than in Cameroon (4.9%), in DR Congo (4.2%), in the Central African Republic (1.2%), and in Gabon (0.54%); but less than in Angola (10.1%).

Comparison with leaders. The Congo's trade was less than in the USA ($1.9 trillion), in Japan ($771.8 billion), in Germany ($296.0

billion), in the United Kingdom ($293.5 billion), and in China ($262.0 billion). The value of trade per capita in Congo was less than in the USA ($6.4 thousand), in Japan ($6.0 thousand), in the UK ($4.9 thousand), in Germany ($3.6 thousand), and in China ($197.5). The growth of trade in Congo was greater than in Germany (1.7%), in the United Kingdom (1.3%), in the United States (1.1%), and in Japan (-0.77%); but less than in China (11.9%).

The 2010s

The value added of trade in Congo was $1.5 billion per year in the 2010s, ranked 138th in the world, and was on a par with Monaco ($1.5 billion). The share in the world was 0.014%, and 0.44% in Africa.

The share of trade in the economy of Congo was 11.0% in the 2010s, ranked 176th in the world, and was on a par with Afghanistan (11.0%), Bolivia (10.9%), Ireland (11.1%).

The trade per capita in Congo was $308.7 in the 2010s, ranked 158th in the world, and was on a par with Ghana ($310.6), Tuvalu ($313.6), Western Africa ($314.3). The Congo's trade per capita was less than trade per capita in the world ($1 436.8) in 4.7 times, and was greater than trade per capita in Africa ($291.7) by 5.8%.

The growth of trade in Congo was 0.2% in the 2010s, ranked 189th in the world. The growth of trade in Congo (0.22%) was less than growth of trade in the world (3.3%), was less than growth of trade in Africa (3.4%).

Comparison with neighbors. The value of trade in Congo was 84.6% higher than in Gabon ($804.7 million) and 4.5 times higher than in the Central African Republic ($331.3 million); but 14.8 times lower than in Angola ($22.1 billion), 4.3 times lower than in Cameroon ($6.4 billion), and 2.7 times lower than in DR Congo ($4.0 billion). The value added of trade per capita in Congo was 11.3% higher than in Cameroon ($277.3), 4.2 times higher than in the Central African Republic ($73.3), and 5.9 times higher than in DR Congo ($52.5); but 2.6 times lower than in Angola ($802.4) and 26.8% lower than in Gabon ($421.9). The growth of trade in Congo was less than in DR Congo (4.9%), in Cameroon (4.4%), in the CAR (3.8%), in Gabon (2.7%), and in Angola (2.5%).

Comparison with leaders. The sector of trade in Congo was 1 761.1 times lower than in the USA ($2.6 trillion), 804.2 times lower than in China ($1.2 trillion), 585.5 times lower than in Japan ($869.5 billion), 250.9 times lower than in Germany ($372.6 billion), and 222.2 times lower than in the UK ($330.0 billion). The value of trade per capita in Congo was 26.5 times lower than in the USA ($8.2 thousand), 22.0 times lower than in Japan ($6.8 thousand), 16.3 times lower than in the UK ($5.0 thousand), 14.7 times lower than in Germany ($4.6 thousand), and 2.8 times lower than in China ($851.7). The growth of trade in Congo was less than in China (8.9%), in the United Kingdom (2.8%), in the USA (2.3%), in Germany (2.0%), and in Japan (0.77%).

Chapter IX. Services

(ISIC J-P)

The services of Congo enlarged from $267.8 million per year in the 1970s to $2.6 billion per year in the 2010s, that is by $2.3 billion or 9.5 times. The change occurred at $1.5 billion due to a 2.5-fold increase in prices, as also at $160.8 million due to a 1.2-fold increase in productivity, as well as at $580.2 million due to the growing in population. The average annual growth in services is 2.9%.   The minimum value of services was in 1970 at $116.2 million. The maximum value of services was in 2014 at $3.1 billion.

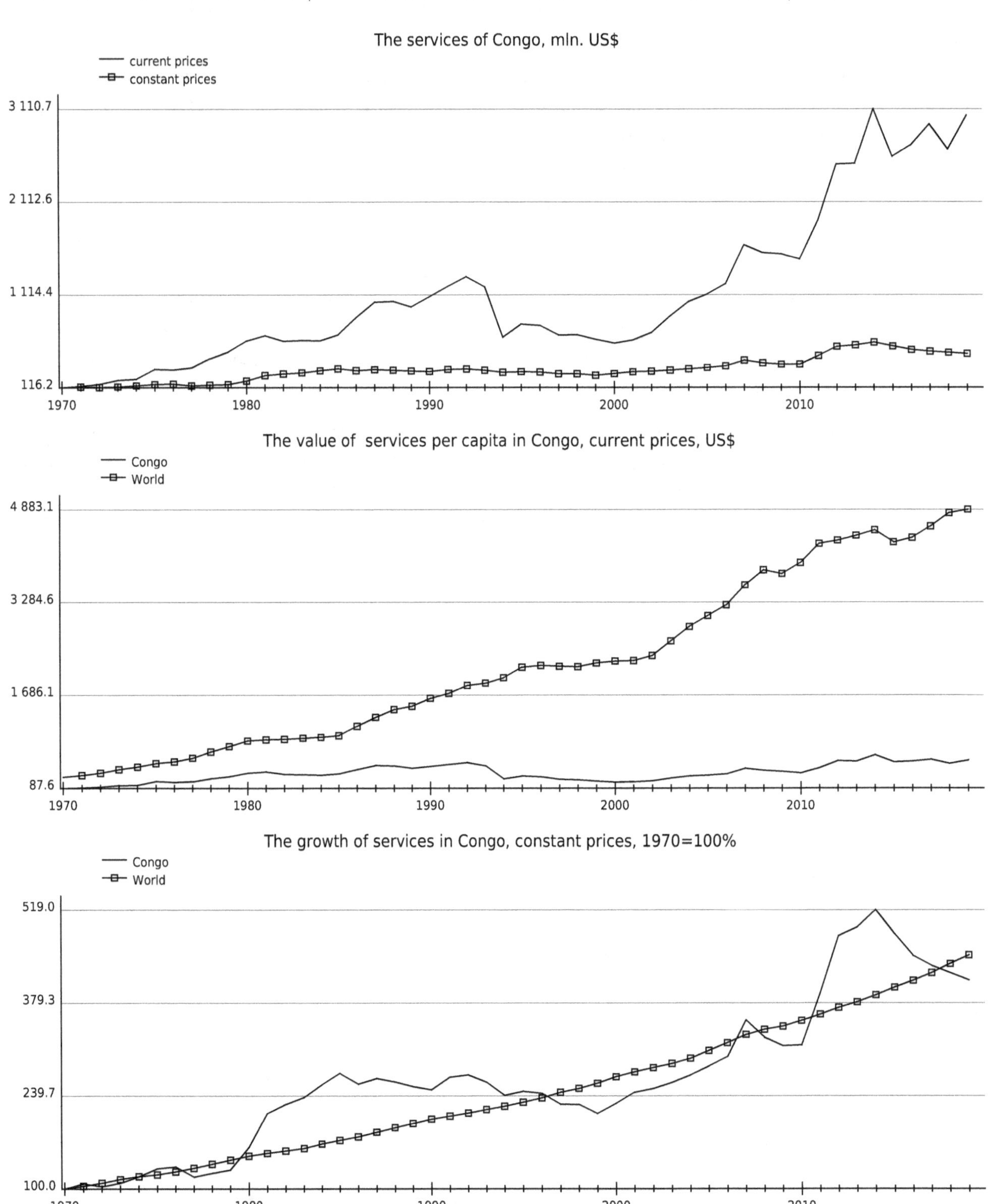

The services of Congo, mln. US$

The value of services per capita in Congo, current prices, US$

The growth of services in Congo, constant prices, 1970=100%

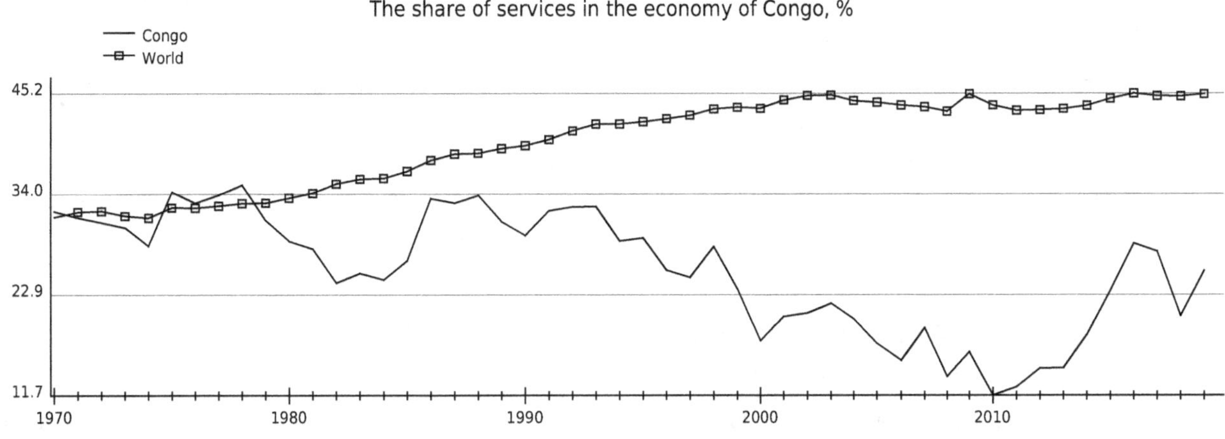

The 1970s

The services of Congo were $267.8 million per year in the 1970s, ranked 111th in the world, and were on a par with Mauritania ($262.4 million). The share in the world was 0.013%, and 0.42% in Africa.

The share of services in the economy of Congo was 32.3% in the 1970s, ranked 61st in the world, and was on a par with the Comoros (32.3%), Cyprus (32.3%), Europe (32.2%).

The services per capita in Congo were $176.2 in the 1970s, ranked 108th in the world, and were on a par with Zimbabwe ($177.3), Guatemala ($172.7), Malaysia ($171.9). The sector of services per capita in Congo was less than services per capita in the world ($506.9) in 2.9 times, and was greater than services per capita in Africa ($156.0) by 13.0%.

The growth of services in Congo was 2.8% in the 1970s, ranked 151st in the world. The growth of services in Congo (2.8%) was less than growth of services in the world (4.1%), was less than growth of services in Africa (5.5%).

Comparison with neighbors. The value of services in Congo was greater than in the CAR ($146.8 million); but less than in DR Congo ($2.0 billion), in Angola ($1.3 billion), in Cameroon ($1.2 billion), and in Gabon ($620.3 million). The value of services per capita in Congo was greater than in Cameroon ($160.2), in DR Congo ($87.4), and in the Central African Republic ($75.0); but less than in Gabon ($962.4) and in Angola ($182.2). The growth of services in Congo was greater than in the CAR (1.4%), in DR Congo (1.0%), and in Angola (0.23%); but less than in Gabon (8.3%) and in Cameroon (5.7%).

Comparison with leaders. The sector of services in Congo was less than in the United States ($674.4 billion), in the USSR ($168.3 billion), in Japan ($153.8 billion), in Germany ($150.2 billion), and in France ($121.8 billion). The value added of services per capita in Congo was less than in the United States ($3.1 thousand), in France ($2.3 thousand), in Germany ($1 907.6), in Japan ($1 381.3), and in the USSR ($667.3). The growth of services in Congo was greater than in the USSR (0.90%); but less than in Japan (5.9%), in Germany (4.8%), in France (3.9%), and in the USA (3.3%).

The 1980s

The value of services in Congo was $777.4 million per year in the 1980s, ranked 107th in the world, and was on a par with Namibia ($768.8 million). The share in the world was 0.014%, and 0.61% in Africa.

The share of services in the economy of Congo was 29.1% in the 1980s, ranked 101st in the world, and was on a par with Trinidad and Tobago (29.2%), Samoa (29.0%), Honduras (29.3%).

The sector of services per capita in Congo was $383.0 in the 1980s, ranked 101st in the world, and was on a par with Vanuatu ($376.1). The sector of services per capita in Congo was less than services per capita in the world ($1 115.5) in 2.9 times, and was greater than services per capita in Africa ($235.7) by 62.5%.

The growth of services in Congo was 7% in the 1980s, ranked 24th in the world. The growth of services in Congo (7.0%) was greater than growth of services in the world (3.3%), was greater than growth of services in Africa (3.9%).

Comparison with neighbors. The services of Congo were greater than in the CAR ($289.4 million); but less than in Cameroon ($3.4 billion), in Angola ($2.4 billion), in Gabon ($1.4 billion), and in DR Congo ($907.1 million). The services per capita in Congo were greater than in Cameroon ($340.3), in Angola ($243.4), in the CAR ($116.1), and in DR Congo ($30.6); but less than in Gabon ($1

650.9). The growth of services in Congo was greater than in the Central African Republic (2.4%), in Cameroon (2.3%), in DR Congo (1.8%), in Angola (1.5%), and in Gabon (1.3%).

Comparison with leaders. The value added of services in Congo was less than in the United States ($1.9 trillion), in Japan ($619.9 billion), in Germany ($362.2 billion), in France ($294.5 billion), and in the United Kingdom ($265.4 billion). The value added of services per capita in Congo was less than in the United States ($7.8 thousand), in France ($5.2 thousand), in Japan ($5.1 thousand), in the UK ($4.7 thousand), and in Germany ($4.6 thousand). The growth of services in Congo was greater than in Japan (4.8%), in the United Kingdom (3.3%), in Germany (3.1%), in the United States (2.8%), and in France (2.3%).

The 1990s

The services of Congo were $903.9 million per year in the 1990s, ranked 132nd in the world, and were on a par with Barbados ($904.7 million). The share in the world was 0.0079%, and 0.59% in Africa.

The share of services in the economy of Congo was 29.1% in the 1990s, ranked 123rd in the world, and was on a par with Lithuania (29.1%), the Solomon Islands (29.2%), Venezuela (28.9%).

The Congo's services per capita were $337.2 in the 1990s, ranked 126th in the world, and were on a par with Northern Africa ($337.0), Algeria ($331.1). The services per capita in Congo were less than services per capita in the world ($2 014.6) in 6.0 times, and were greater than services per capita in Africa ($217.8) by 54.8%.

The growth of services in Congo was -1.7% in the 1990s, ranked 187th in the world. The growth of services in Congo (-1.7%) was less than growth of services in the world (2.7%), was less than growth of services in Africa (2.6%).

Comparison with neighbors. The services of Congo were greater than in DR Congo ($830.7 million) and in the Central African Republic ($271.0 million); but less than in Cameroon ($3.3 billion), in Angola ($2.2 billion), and in Gabon ($1.4 billion). The sector of services per capita in Congo was greater than in Cameroon ($242.4), in Angola ($162.5), in the Central African Republic ($85.2), and in DR Congo ($20.5); but less than in Gabon ($1 329.9). The growth of services in Congo was greater than in Angola (-2.2%) and in DR Congo (-2.5%); but less than in Gabon (3.1%), in Cameroon (1.3%), and in the CAR (0.93%).

Comparison with leaders. The value added of services in Congo was less than in the USA ($3.8 trillion), in Japan ($1.6 trillion), in Germany ($908.0 billion), in France ($628.2 billion), and in the UK ($592.3 billion). The value added of services per capita in Congo was less than in the USA ($14.4 thousand), in Japan ($12.8 thousand), in Germany ($11.3 thousand), in France ($10.6 thousand), and in the UK ($10.2 thousand). The growth of services in Congo was less than in Germany (3.2%), in the United Kingdom (3.0%), in the USA (2.3%), in Japan (1.7%), and in France (1.6%).

The 2000s

The value added of services in Congo was $1.1 billion per year in the 2000s, ranked 146th in the world, and was on a par with Aruba ($1.1 billion), Moldova ($1.1 billion). The share in the world was 0.0056%, and 0.39% in Africa.

The share of services in the economy of Congo was 17.5% in the 2000s, ranked 194th in the world, and was on a par with Uzbekistan (17.4%), Tajikistan (17.4%).

The value of services per capita in Congo was $305.1 in the 2000s, ranked 151st in the world, and was on a par with Senegal ($301.0), Nigeria ($300.3), Papua New Guinea ($299.2). The Congo's services per capita were less than services per capita in the world ($3 011.2) in 9.9 times, and were less than services per capita in Africa ($314.3) by 2.9%.

The growth of services in Congo was 4% in the 2000s, ranked 100th in the world, and was on a par with Yemen (4.0%), Lebanon (4.0%), the Cook Islands (4.0%). The growth of services in Congo (4.0%) was greater than growth of services in the world (2.9%), was less than growth of services in Africa (5.1%).

Comparison with neighbors. The value of services in Congo was greater than in the CAR ($271.3 million); but less than in Angola ($8.2 billion), in Cameroon ($4.4 billion), in Gabon ($2.1 billion), and in DR Congo ($1.8 billion). The sector of services per capita in Congo was greater than in Cameroon ($252.6), in the CAR ($67.9), and in DR Congo ($33.1); but less than in Gabon ($1 527.9) and in Angola ($425.7). The growth of services in Congo was greater than in DR Congo (2.3%) and in the CAR (-3.0%); but less than in Cameroon (5.0%), in Angola (4.8%), and in Gabon (4.0%).

Comparison with leaders. The value added of services in Congo was less than in the United States ($6.7 trillion), in Japan ($2.0 trillion), in Germany ($1.2 trillion), in the United Kingdom ($1.1 trillion), and in France ($997.0 billion). The value of services per capita in Congo was less than in the USA ($22.9 thousand), in the United Kingdom ($18.0 thousand), in France ($15.9 thousand), in Japan ($15.3 thousand), and in Germany ($15.0 thousand). The growth of services in Congo was greater than in the UK (2.7%), in the USA (2.0%), in France (1.5%), in Japan (1.2%), and in Germany (0.57%).

The 2010s

The services of Congo were $2.6 billion per year in the 2010s, ranked 148th in the world, and were on a par with Rwanda ($2.6 billion). The share in the world was 0.0078%, and 0.41% in Africa.

The share of services in the economy of Congo was 18.9% in the 2010s, ranked 196th in the world, and was on a par with Equatorial Guinea (18.7%), Ghana (18.7%).

The value added of services per capita in Congo was $531.1 in the 2010s, ranked 159th in the world, and was on a par with Côte d'Ivoire ($533.1), Africa ($528.2), Timor-Leste ($524.4). The services per capita in Congo were less than services per capita in the world ($4 467.8) in 8.4 times, and were greater than services per capita in Africa ($528.2) by 0.54%.

The growth of services in Congo was 2.8% in the 2010s, ranked 109th in the world, and was on a par with the World (2.7%). The growth of services in Congo (2.8%) was greater than growth of services in the world (2.7%), was less than growth of services in Africa (3.4%).

Comparison with neighbors. The value added of services in Congo was 6.0 times higher than in the Central African Republic ($425.3 million); but 8.9 times lower than in Angola ($22.8 billion), 3.2 times lower than in Cameroon ($8.2 billion), 44.7% lower than in DR Congo ($4.6 billion), and 41.3% lower than in Gabon ($4.4 billion). The Congo's services per capita were 49.6% higher than in Cameroon ($354.9), 5.6 times higher than in the Central African Republic ($94.1), and 8.7 times higher than in DR Congo ($61.3); but 4.3 times lower than in Gabon ($2.3 thousand) and 36.0% lower than in Angola ($830.0). The growth of services in Congo was greater than in Angola (1.4%) and in the Central African Republic (-3.1%); but less than in Gabon (5.5%), in Cameroon (4.4%), and in DR Congo (3.6%).

Comparison with leaders. The Congo's services were 3 896.3 times lower than in the USA ($10.0 trillion), 1 388.3 times lower than in China ($3.5 trillion), 889.8 times lower than in Japan ($2.3 trillion), 629.1 times lower than in Germany ($1.6 trillion), and 530.5 times lower than in the United Kingdom ($1.4 trillion). The services per capita in Congo were 58.7 times lower than in the USA ($31.2 thousand), 38.9 times lower than in the United Kingdom ($20.7 thousand), 37.0 times lower than in Germany ($19.6 thousand), 33.5 times lower than in Japan ($17.8 thousand), and 4.8 times lower than in China ($2.5 thousand). The growth of services in Congo was greater than in the USA (1.8%), in the United Kingdom (1.7%), in Germany (1.2%), and in Japan (0.99%); but less than in China (8.4%).

Part III. External relations

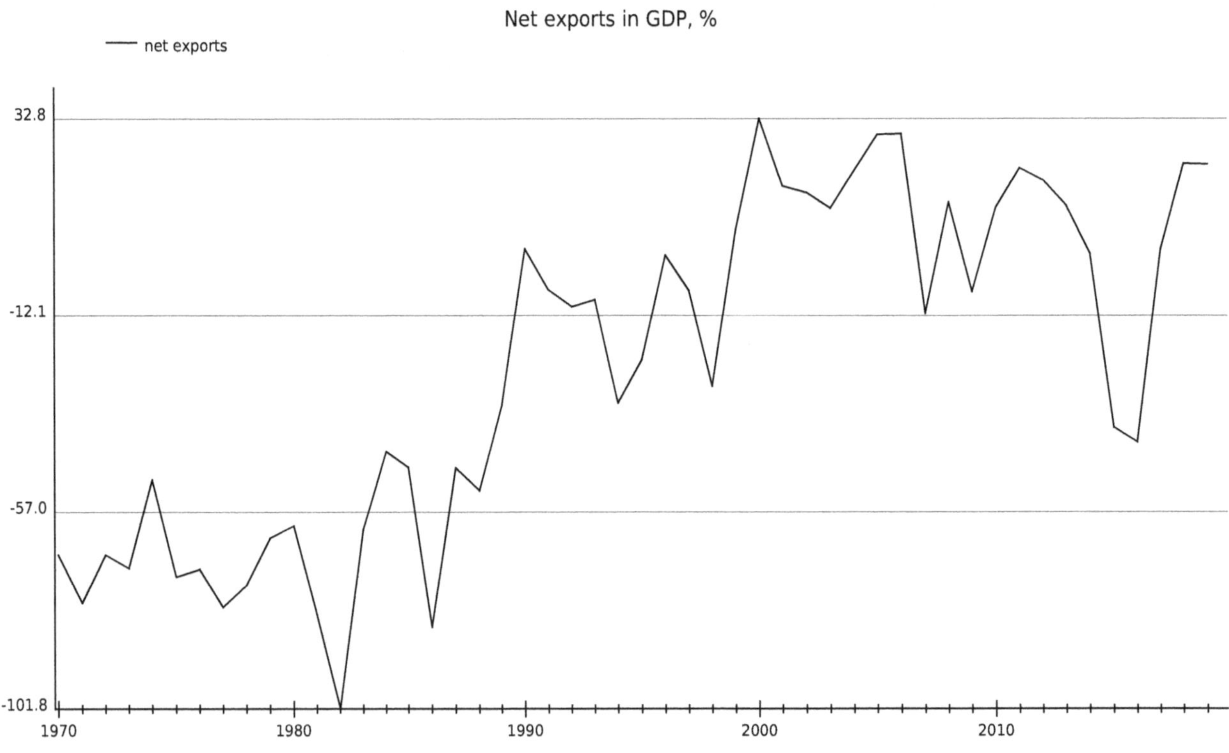

Chapter X. Exports

Exports of goods and services

The value of exports from Congo grew up from $270.6 million per year in the 1970s to $8.4 billion per year in the 2010s, that is by $8.2 billion or 31.2 times. The change occurred at $7.2 billion due to a 6.9-fold increase in prices, as also at $368.8 million due to a 1.4-fold increase in per capita rate, as well as at $586.3 million due to the growth in population. The average annual growth in exports is 4.4%. The minimum value of exports was in 1970 at $83.1 million. The maximum value of exports was in 2011 at $11.5 billion.

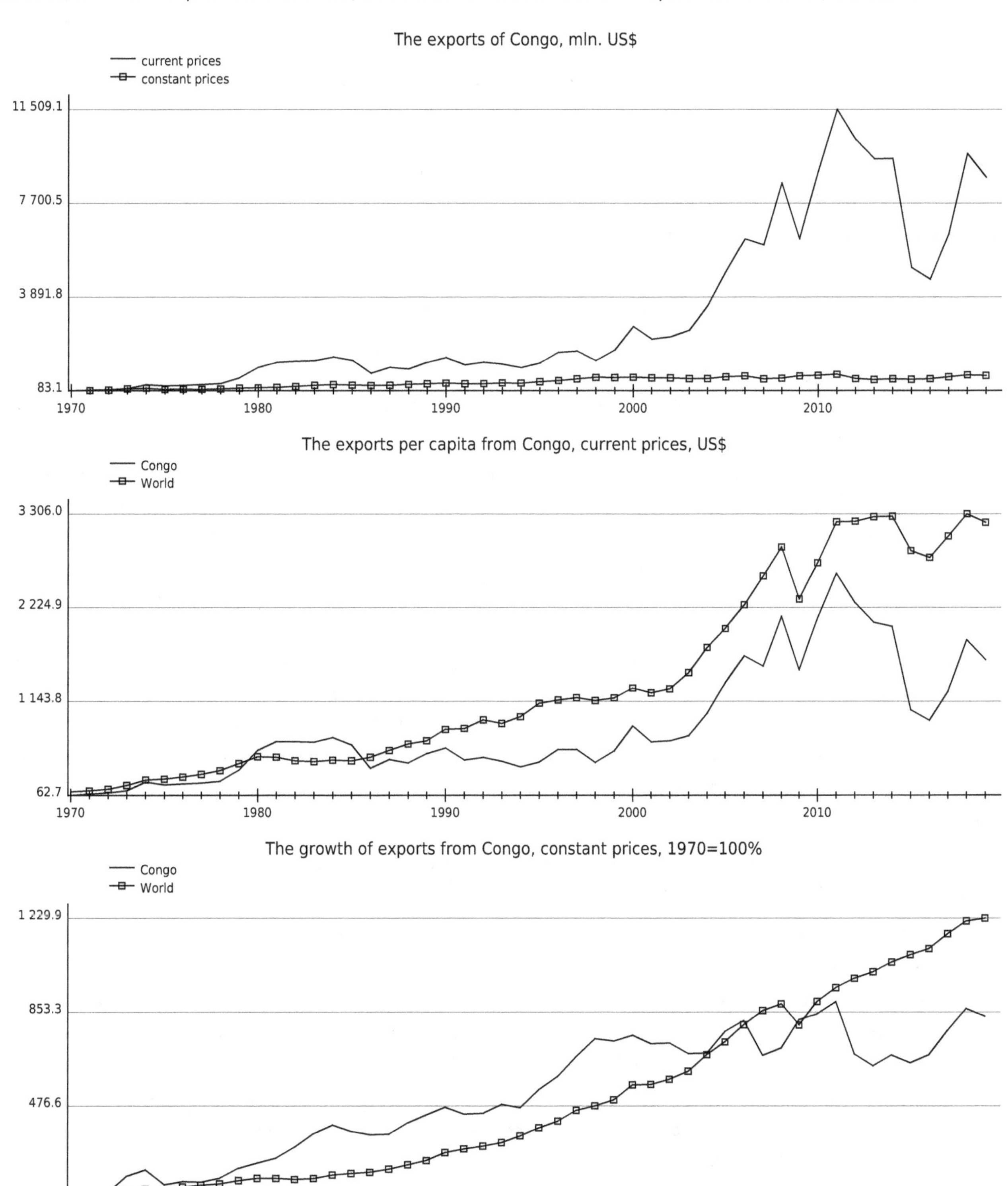

The exports of Congo, mln. US$

The exports per capita from Congo, current prices, US$

The growth of exports from Congo, constant prices, 1970=100%

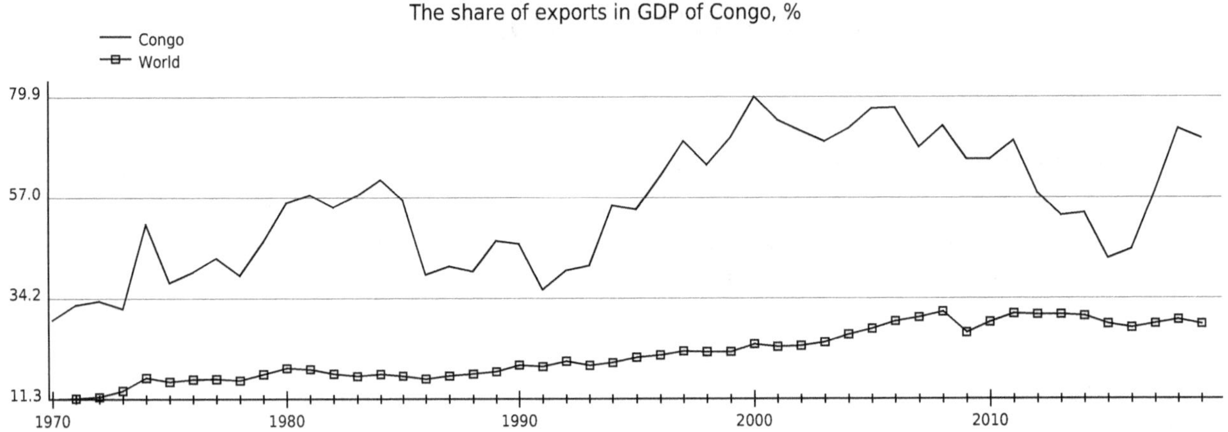

The 1970s

The exports of Congo were $270.6 million per year in the 1970s, ranked 112th in the world, and were on a par with New Caledonia ($270.2 million). The share in the world was 0.028%, and 0.48% from Africa.

The share of exports in GDP of Congo was 40.6% in the 1970s, ranked 55th in the world, and was on a par with Melanesia (40.8%).

The Congo's exports per capita were $178.1 in the 1970s, ranked 105th in the world, and were on a par with Dominica ($176.4), South Korea ($180.6). The Congo's exports per capita were less than exports per capita in the world ($242.1) by 26.4%, and were greater than exports per capita from Africa ($137.0) by 30.0%.

The growth of exports from Congo was 9.5% in the 1970s, ranked 35th in the world, and was on a par with the Cayman Islands (9.4%), DR Congo (9.4%). The growth of exports from Congo (9.5%) was greater than growth of exports in the world (6.5%), was greater than growth of exports from Africa (5.7%).

Comparison with neighbors. The Congo's exports were greater than from the Central African Republic ($137.4 million); but less than from DR Congo ($3.0 billion), from Angola ($1.6 billion), from Cameroon ($1.1 billion), and from Gabon ($958.5 million). The Congo's exports per capita were greater than from Cameroon ($154.5), from DR Congo ($130.6), and from the Central African Republic ($70.3); but less than from Gabon ($1 487.2) and from Angola ($232.2). The growth of exports from Congo was greater than from DR Congo (9.4%), from Gabon (8.1%), from Angola (0.24%), and from the Central African Republic (-2.9%); but less than from Cameroon (13.1%).

Comparison with leaders. The value of exports from Congo was less than from the United States ($128.0 billion), from Germany ($82.9 billion), from France ($64.3 billion), from Japan ($64.1 billion), and from the UK ($61.3 billion). The Congo's exports per capita were less than from France ($1 199.1), from the UK ($1 094.1), from Germany ($1 052.2), from the USA ($586.5), and from Japan ($575.8). The growth of exports from Congo was greater than from Japan (8.6%), from France (7.8%), from the United States (6.8%), from Germany (5.1%), and from the United Kingdom (5.0%).

The 1980s

The Congo's exports were $1.2 billion per year in the 1980s, ranked 94th in the world, and were on a par with San Marino ($1.2 billion). The share in the world was 0.046%, and 1.1% from Africa.

The share of exports in GDP of Congo was 51.1% in the 1980s, ranked 34th in the world, and was on a par with Ireland (51.1%), Barbados (51.0%), Anguilla (50.9%).

The value of exports per capita from Congo was $574.6 in the 1980s, ranked 86th in the world, and was on a par with Dominica ($567.9), the Marshall Islands ($583.9). The Congo's exports per capita were greater than exports per capita in the world ($529.9) by 8.4%, and were greater than exports per capita from Africa ($201.4) in 2.9 times.

The growth of exports from Congo was 6.9% in the 1980s, ranked 41st in the world, and was on a par with Côte d'Ivoire (6.9%), Saint Lucia (6.9%), South-Eastern Asia (6.9%). The growth of exports from Congo (6.9%) was greater than growth of exports in the world (3.8%), was greater than growth of exports from Africa (-0.87%).

Comparison with neighbors. The Congo's exports were greater than from the CAR ($239.7 million); but less than from DR Congo ($4.3

billion), from Angola ($2.8 billion), from Cameroon ($2.7 billion), and from Gabon ($2.0 billion). The value of exports per capita from Congo was greater than from Angola ($286.9), from Cameroon ($269.6), from DR Congo ($146.3), and from the Central African Republic ($96.2); but less than from Gabon ($2.5 thousand). The growth of exports from Congo was greater than from Angola (6.4%), from the CAR (5.1%), from Gabon (3.5%), and from Cameroon (-0.068%); but less than from DR Congo (8.5%).

Comparison with leaders. The Congo's exports were less than from the USA ($338.6 billion), from Japan ($210.6 billion), from Germany ($208.1 billion), from France ($155.9 billion), and from the United Kingdom ($155.0 billion). The value of exports per capita from Congo was less than from France ($2.8 thousand), from the UK ($2.7 thousand), from Germany ($2.7 thousand), from Japan ($1 736.5), and from the USA ($1 413.8). The growth of exports from Congo was greater than from Japan (6.7%), from the United States (5.7%), from Germany (4.7%), from France (4.0%), and from the UK (3.0%).

The 1990s

The Congo's exports were $1.4 billion per year in the 1990s, ranked 115th in the world, and were on a par with Bolivia ($1.4 billion). The share in the world was 0.023%, and 0.95% from Africa.

The share of exports in GDP of Congo was 52.8% in the 1990s, ranked 38th in the world, and was on a par with Saint Lucia (52.7%), Belize (52.7%), Belarus (53.2%).

The value of exports per capita from Congo was $505.7 in the 1990s, ranked 114th in the world, and was on a par with Nauru ($503.7), Equatorial Guinea ($508.4), the Solomon Islands ($517.8). The exports per capita from Congo were less than exports per capita in the world ($1 029.5) in 2.0 times, and were greater than exports per capita from Africa ($202.1) in 2.5 times.

The growth of exports from Congo was 5.3% in the 1990s, ranked 101st in the world, and was on a par with Western Asia (5.2%), Cyprus (5.3%), Austria (5.3%). The growth of exports from Congo (5.3%) was less than growth of exports in the world (6.9%), was greater than growth of exports from Africa (2.5%).

Comparison with neighbors. The Congo's exports were greater than from the CAR ($258.4 million); but less than from Angola ($7.3 billion), from Cameroon ($2.9 billion), from Gabon ($2.8 billion), and from DR Congo ($2.5 billion). The Congo's exports per capita were greater than from Cameroon ($214.3), from the CAR ($81.3), and from DR Congo ($62.6); but less than from Gabon ($2.6 thousand) and from Angola ($526.3). The growth of exports from Congo was greater than from Gabon (3.3%), from DR Congo (3.3%), and from the Central African Republic (-0.54%); but less than from Angola (9.7%) and from Cameroon (8.0%).

Comparison with leaders. The Congo's exports were less than from the United States ($773.6 billion), from Germany ($509.0 billion), from Japan ($418.7 billion), from France ($329.8 billion), and from the UK ($324.3 billion). The value of exports per capita from Congo was less than from Germany ($6.3 thousand), from the UK ($5.6 thousand), from France ($5.6 thousand), from Japan ($3.3 thousand), and from the USA ($2.9 thousand). The growth of exports from Congo was greater than from Japan (4.2%); but less than from the United States (7.2%), from France (6.5%), from Germany (6.0%), and from the United Kingdom (5.7%).

The 2000s

The exports of Congo were $4.5 billion per year in the 2000s, ranked 106th in the world, and were on a par with Cameroon ($4.5 billion). The share in the world was 0.036%, and 1.2% from Africa.

The structure of exports: primary products (82.2%), resource-based manufactures (12.7%), and medium technology manufactures (3.8%).

Congo exported goods to China (28.4%), the USA (25.5%), Taiwan (11.9%), Republic of Korea (6.5%), France (4.4%) and other countries (23.4%).

The share of exports in GDP of Congo was 72.6% in the 2000s, ranked 18th in the world, and was on a par with Slovakia (72.6%), the Cook Islands (72.4%), the Maldives (72.4%).

The exports per capita from Congo were $1 254.8 in the 2000s, ranked 112th in the world, and were on a par with Jordan ($1 230.0), Argentina ($1 229.8), Algeria ($1 281.2). The value of exports per capita from Congo was less than exports per capita in the world ($1 933.7) by 35.1%, and was greater than exports per capita from Africa ($398.4) in 3.1 times.

The growth of exports from Congo was 1.1% in the 2000s, ranked 175th in the world, and was on a par with Syria (1.1%). The growth of exports from Congo (1.1%) was less than growth of exports in the world (4.8%), was less than growth of exports from Africa (5.3%).

Comparison with neighbors. The value of exports from Congo was greater than from Cameroon ($4.5 billion), from DR Congo ($3.3 billion), and from the CAR ($216.9 million); but less than from Angola ($25.7 billion) and from Gabon ($5.2 billion). The value of exports per capita from Congo was greater than from Cameroon ($256.4), from DR Congo ($60.7), and from the Central African Republic ($54.2); but less than from Gabon ($3.7 thousand) and from Angola ($1 333.6). The growth of exports from Congo was greater than from Gabon (-2.4%) and from the Central African Republic (-3.9%); but less than from Angola (7.6%), from DR Congo (5.0%), and from Cameroon (1.2%).

Comparison with leaders. The Congo's exports were less than from the USA ($1.3 trillion), from Germany ($1.0 trillion), from China ($780.2 billion), from Japan ($626.3 billion), and from the United Kingdom ($591.1 billion). The Congo's exports per capita were greater than from China ($588.1); but less than from Germany ($12.8 thousand), from the UK ($9.8 thousand), from Japan ($4.9 thousand), and from the USA ($4.5 thousand). The growth of exports from Congo was less than from China (12.7%), from Germany (5.0%), from Japan (3.5%), from the USA (3.3%), and from the UK (2.8%).

The 2010s

The value of exports from Congo was $8.4 billion per year in the 2010s, ranked 111th in the world, and was on a par with Tanzania ($8.5 billion), Gabon ($8.6 billion). The share in the world was 0.037%, and 1.4% from Africa.

The structure of exports: primary products (78.5%), resource-based manufactures (7.2%), and medium technology manufactures (12.3%).

Congo exported goods to China (39.3%), the United States (10.1%), Australia (5.0%), France (4.9%), Italy (4.6%) and other countries (36.2%).

The share of exports in GDP of Congo was 59.3% in the 2010s, ranked 46th in the world, and was on a par with Latvia (59.8%), Oman (58.7%).

The value of exports per capita from Congo was $1 753.6 in the 2010s, ranked 117th in the world, and was on a par with Tunisia ($1 767.0), Venezuela ($1 777.6), Central Asia ($1 711.9). The value of exports per capita from Congo was less than exports per capita in the world ($3 098.9) by 43.4%, and was greater than exports per capita from Africa ($534.3) in 3.3 times.

The growth of exports from Congo was 0.2% in the 2010s, ranked 186th in the world. The growth of exports from Congo (0.16%) was less than growth of exports in the world (4.4%), was greater than growth of exports from Africa (-1.2%).

Comparison with neighbors. The Congo's exports were 15.7% higher than from Cameroon ($7.3 billion) and 26.5 times higher than from the Central African Republic ($317.8 million); but 5.9 times lower than from Angola ($50.1 billion), 28.1% lower than from DR Congo ($11.7 billion), and 1.7% lower than from Gabon ($8.6 billion). The Congo's exports per capita were 5.5 times higher than from Cameroon ($316.6), 11.3 times higher than from DR Congo ($155.8), and 24.9 times higher than from the Central African Republic ($70.3); but 2.6 times lower than from Gabon ($4.5 thousand) and 3.9% lower than from Angola ($1 824.3). The growth of exports from Congo was greater than from Angola (-2.4%); but less than from DR Congo (12.8%), from the Central African Republic (10.2%), from Cameroon (4.3%), and from Gabon (3.0%).

Comparison with leaders. The exports of Congo were 271.8 times lower than from China ($2.3 trillion), 269.0 times lower than from the United States ($2.3 trillion), 199.5 times lower than from Germany ($1.7 trillion), 101.9 times lower than from Japan ($859.4 billion), and 96.6 times lower than from the United Kingdom ($815.1 billion). The value of exports per capita from Congo was 7.2% higher than from China ($1 635.3); but 11.7 times lower than from Germany ($20.6 thousand), 7.1 times lower than from the UK ($12.4 thousand), 4.1 times lower than from the USA ($7.1 thousand), and 3.8 times lower than from Japan ($6.7 thousand). The growth of exports from Congo was less than from China (6.8%), from Germany (4.7%), from Japan (4.6%), from the USA (3.7%), and from the United Kingdom (3.1%).

Chapter XI. Imports

Imports of goods and services

The Congo's imports grew up from $726.5 million per year in the 1970s to $7.6 billion per year in the 2010s, that is by $6.8 billion or 10.4 times. The change occurred at $2.1 billion due to a 1.4-fold increase in prices, as also at $3.1 billion due to a 2.4-fold increase in per capita rate, as well as at $1.6 billion due to the expansion in population. The average annual growth in imports is 4.7%. The minimum value of imports was in 1970 at $272.3 million. The maximum value of imports was in 2015 at $9.5 billion.

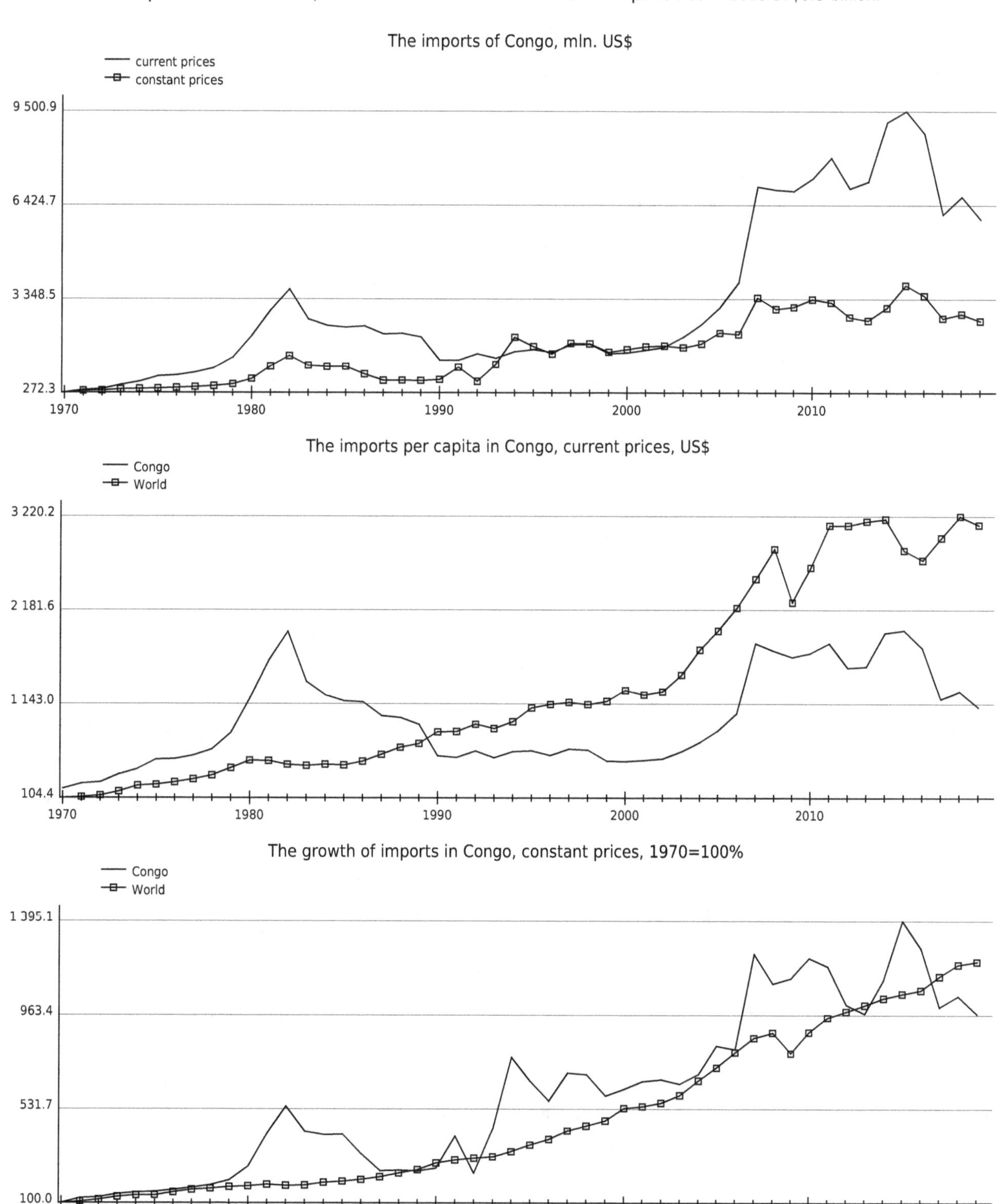

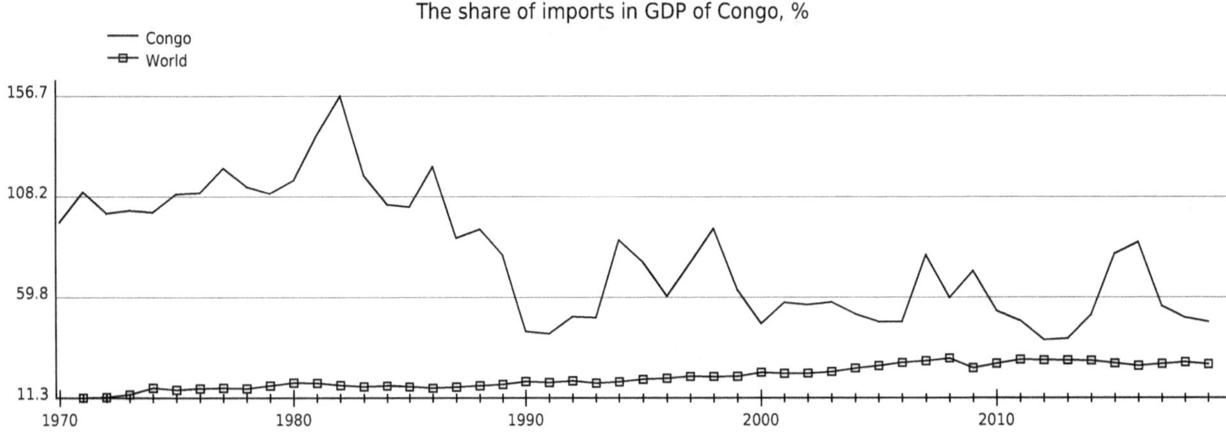

The 1970s

The value of imports in Congo was $726.5 million per year in the 1970s, ranked 88th in the world, and was on a par with Qatar ($727.6 million), Jamaica ($743.6 million). The share in the world was 0.074%, and 1.2% in Africa.

The share of imports in GDP of Congo was 109.1% in the 1970s, ranked 5th in the world.

The imports per capita in Congo were $478.2 in the 1970s, ranked 76th in the world, and were on a par with Costa Rica ($479.2), Fiji ($477.0), Western Asia ($468.1). The imports per capita in Congo were greater than imports per capita in the world ($244.3) by 95.7%, and were greater than imports per capita in Africa ($142.6) in 3.4 times.

The growth of imports in Congo was 8.2% in the 1970s, ranked 51st in the world, and was on a par with Malta (8.2%), Southern Asia (8.2%), El Salvador (8.3%). The growth of imports in Congo (8.2%) was greater than growth of imports in the world (6.3%), was greater than growth of imports in Africa (6.7%).

Comparison with neighbors. The imports of Congo were greater than in the CAR ($199.0 million); but less than in DR Congo ($3.9 billion), in Cameroon ($1.5 billion), in Angola ($1.5 billion), and in Gabon ($820.6 million). The value of imports per capita in Congo was greater than in Angola ($218.0), in Cameroon ($206.3), in DR Congo ($172.0), and in the Central African Republic ($101.7); but less than in Gabon ($1 273.2). The growth of imports in Congo was greater than in DR Congo (8.0%), in Angola (0.40%), and in the Central African Republic (-0.87%); but less than in Cameroon (13.8%) and in Gabon (11.4%).

Comparison with leaders. The imports of Congo were less than in the USA ($133.2 billion), in Germany ($92.5 billion), in France ($63.3 billion), in the UK ($62.4 billion), and in Japan ($61.0 billion). The imports per capita in Congo were less than in France ($1 181.1), in Germany ($1 175.1), in the United Kingdom ($1 113.2), in the USA ($610.4), and in Japan ($547.6). The growth of imports in Congo was greater than in France (7.2%), in Japan (7.0%), in Germany (5.6%), in the USA (5.1%), and in the United Kingdom (4.5%).

The 1980s

The value of imports in Congo was $2.5 billion per year in the 1980s, ranked 74th in the world, and was on a par with Cyprus ($2.5 billion). The share in the world was 0.097%, and 2.2% in Africa.

The share of imports in GDP of Congo was 111.0% in the 1980s, ranked 6th in the world.

The imports per capita in Congo were $1 248.2 in the 1980s, ranked 67th in the world, and were on a par with the Caribbean ($1 255.0), Spain ($1 258.3), Iraq ($1 237.0). The Congo's imports per capita were greater than imports per capita in the world ($539.1) in 2.3 times, and were greater than imports per capita in Africa ($208.0) in 6.0 times.

The growth of imports in Congo was 1.9% in the 1980s, ranked 116th in the world. The growth of imports in Congo (1.9%) was less than growth of imports in the world (3.8%), was greater than growth of imports in Africa (-3.1%).

Comparison with neighbors. The imports of Congo were greater than in Angola ($2.5 billion), in Gabon ($1.6 billion), and in the CAR ($350.1 million); but less than in DR Congo ($4.2 billion) and in Cameroon ($3.2 billion). The imports per capita in Congo were greater than in Cameroon ($324.6), in Angola ($250.5), in DR Congo ($140.8), and in the Central African Republic ($140.5); but less than in Gabon ($1 943.8). The growth of imports in Congo was greater than in Angola (-1.3%) and in Cameroon (-4.2%); but less than in DR Congo (12.1%), in the Central African Republic (4.8%), and in Gabon (2.4%).

Comparison with leaders. The value of imports in Congo was less than in the United States ($417.2 billion), in Germany ($225.6 billion), in Japan ($175.9 billion), in France ($162.0 billion), and in the UK ($157.7 billion). The imports per capita in Congo were less than in Germany ($2.9 thousand), in France ($2.9 thousand), in the UK ($2.8 thousand), in the United States ($1 742.4), and in Japan ($1 450.4). The growth of imports in Congo was less than in the USA (5.8%), in the United Kingdom (5.1%), in Japan (4.6%), in France (4.3%), and in Germany (3.3%).

The 1990s

The Congo's imports were $1.6 billion per year in the 1990s, ranked 122nd in the world, and were on a par with Zambia ($1.6 billion). The share in the world was 0.027%, and 1.1% in Africa.

The share of imports in GDP of Congo was 61.5% in the 1990s, ranked 39th in the world, and was on a par with Tuvalu (61.3%).

The imports per capita in Congo were $589.1 in the 1990s, ranked 124th in the world, and were on a par with Eastern Asia ($591.9), Papua New Guinea ($582.4), Macedonia ($602.9). The imports per capita in Congo were less than imports per capita in the world ($1 015.5) by 42.0%, and were greater than imports per capita in Africa ($211.4) in 2.8 times.

The growth of imports in Congo was 9.1% in the 1990s, ranked 37th in the world, and was on a par with Spain (9.1%), South America (9.1%), Guatemala (9.1%). The growth of imports in Congo (9.1%) was greater than growth of imports in the world (6.6%), was greater than growth of imports in Africa (3.8%).

Comparison with neighbors. The value of imports in Congo was greater than in the Central African Republic ($324.4 million); but less than in Angola ($7.1 billion), in Cameroon ($2.6 billion), in DR Congo ($2.4 billion), and in Gabon ($1.8 billion). The Congo's imports per capita were greater than in Angola ($515.4), in Cameroon ($191.8), in the CAR ($102.0), and in DR Congo ($58.9); but less than in Gabon ($1 656.9). The growth of imports in Congo was greater than in Cameroon (9.0%), in DR Congo (0.49%), in the Central African Republic (-0.14%), and in Gabon (-0.69%); but less than in Angola (12.8%).

Comparison with leaders. The value of imports in Congo was less than in the United States ($874.1 billion), in Germany ($501.6 billion), in Japan ($355.9 billion), in the United Kingdom ($330.2 billion), and in France ($308.5 billion). The imports per capita in Congo were less than in Germany ($6.2 thousand), in the United Kingdom ($5.7 thousand), in France ($5.2 thousand), in the United States ($3.3 thousand), and in Japan ($2.8 thousand). The growth of imports in Congo was greater than in the United States (8.3%), in Germany (6.4%), in France (5.1%), in the UK (5.1%), and in Japan (3.3%).

The 2000s

The imports of Congo were $3.7 billion per year in the 2000s, ranked 115th in the world, and were on a par with Afghanistan ($3.7 billion), Senegal ($3.7 billion), Albania ($3.8 billion). The share in the world was 0.030%, and 1.1% in Africa.

The structure of imports: primary products (8.2%), resource-based manufactures (16.1%), low technology manufactures (13.4%), medium technology manufactures (49.5%), and high technology manufactures (11.1%).

Congo imported goods from France (17.8%), China (9.6%), Italy (6.5%), the United States (5.7%), India (4.9%) and other countries (55.5%).

The share of imports in GDP of Congo was 60.1% in the 2000s, ranked 53rd in the world, and was on a par with Slovenia (60.2%), Lithuania (60.1%), Mauritius (60.2%).

The Congo's imports per capita were $1 040.1 in the 2000s, ranked 125th in the world, and were on a par with Kiribati ($1 053.5), Kosovo ($1 058.9). The imports per capita in Congo were less than imports per capita in the world ($1 899.9) by 45.3%, and were greater than imports per capita in Africa ($369.3) in 2.8 times.

The growth of imports in Congo was 6.7% in the 2000s, ranked 76th in the world, and was on a par with Kiribati (6.7%). The growth of imports in Congo (6.7%) was greater than growth of imports in the world (5.1%), was less than growth of imports in Africa (7.6%).

Comparison with neighbors. The imports of Congo were greater than in Gabon ($2.5 billion) and in the CAR ($324.4 million); but less than in Angola ($18.8 billion), in Cameroon ($4.8 billion), and in DR Congo ($3.9 billion). The value of imports per capita in Congo was greater than in Angola ($977.0), in Cameroon ($274.2), in the Central African Republic ($81.1), and in DR Congo ($71.4); but less than in Gabon ($1 813.4). The growth of imports in Congo was greater than in Cameroon (4.5%), in Angola (3.8%), in Gabon (2.3%), and in the CAR (-0.55%); but less than in DR Congo (12.8%).

Comparison with leaders. The imports of Congo were less than in the United States ($1.9 trillion), in Germany ($914.7 billion), in the United Kingdom ($641.8 billion), in China ($641.1 billion), and in Japan ($566.4 billion). The imports per capita in Congo were greater than in China ($483.3); but less than in Germany ($11.2 thousand), in the UK ($10.6 thousand), in the United States ($6.4 thousand), and in Japan ($4.4 thousand). The growth of imports in Congo was greater than in Germany (3.7%), in the UK (3.1%), in the USA (2.8%), and in Japan (1.8%); but less than in China (15.1%).

The 2010s

The value of imports in Congo was $7.6 billion per year in the 2010s, ranked 119th in the world, and was on a par with Uganda ($7.6 billion). The share in the world was 0.034%, and 1.1% in Africa.

The structure of imports: primary products (8.2%), resource-based manufactures (14.0%), low technology manufactures (10.8%), medium technology manufactures (57.9%), and high technology manufactures (7.8%).

Congo imported goods from China (13.7%), France (13.3%), South Korea (4.9%), Italy (4.6%), the United States (4.4%) and other countries (59.2%).

The share of imports in GDP of Congo was 53.2% in the 2010s, ranked 84th in the world, and was on a par with Tajikistan (53.2%), Kosovo (53.4%), Palestine (52.8%).

The value of imports per capita in Congo was $1 571.6 in the 2010s, ranked 136th in the world, and was on a par with Ecuador ($1 564.3), Kiribati ($1 558.7), Peru ($1 533.8). The imports per capita in Congo were less than imports per capita in the world ($3 015.6) by 47.9%, and were greater than imports per capita in Africa ($592.1) in 2.7 times.

The growth of imports in Congo was -1.6% in the 2010s, ranked 199th in the world. The growth of imports in Congo (-1.6%) was less than growth of imports in the world (4.4%), was less than growth of imports in Africa (2.0%).

Comparison with neighbors. The imports of Congo were 67.9% higher than in Gabon ($4.5 billion) and 11.1 times higher than in the CAR ($682.0 million); but 4.9 times lower than in Angola ($36.9 billion), 44.0% lower than in DR Congo ($13.5 billion), and 14.8% lower than in Cameroon ($8.9 billion). The value of imports per capita in Congo was 17.1% higher than in Angola ($1 341.8), 4.1 times higher than in Cameroon ($385.1), 8.8 times higher than in DR Congo ($179.5), and 10.4 times higher than in the Central African Republic ($150.9); but 33.5% lower than in Gabon ($2.4 thousand). The growth of imports in Congo was greater than in Angola (-6.4%); but less than in DR Congo (10.6%), in the Central African Republic (7.0%), in Cameroon (5.4%), and in Gabon (3.6%).

Comparison with leaders. The value of imports in Congo was 372.6 times lower than in the United States ($2.8 trillion), 273.7 times lower than in China ($2.1 trillion), 192.4 times lower than in Germany ($1.5 trillion), 116.1 times lower than in Japan ($877.9 billion), and 113.1 times lower than in the United Kingdom ($854.8 billion). The Congo's imports per capita were 6.5% higher than in China ($1 475.4); but 11.3 times lower than in Germany ($17.8 thousand), 8.3 times lower than in the United Kingdom ($13.0 thousand), 5.6 times lower than in the USA ($8.8 thousand), and 4.4 times lower than in Japan ($6.9 thousand). The growth of imports in Congo was less than in China (8.2%), in Germany (4.8%), in the USA (4.4%), in Japan (3.8%), and in the United Kingdom (3.6%).

Part IV. Consumption

Chapter XII. Government consumption expenditure

General government final consumption expenditure

The government expenditure of Congo grew from $151.2 million per year in the 1970s to $2.2 billion per year in the 2010s, that is by $2.1 billion or 14.7 times. The change occurred at $1.7 billion due to a 4.1-fold increase in prices, as also at $59.0 million due to a 1.1-fold increase in per capita rate, as well as at $327.7 million due to the growing in population. The average annual growth in government expenditure is 2.7%. The minimum value of government expenditure was in 1970 at $61.9 million. The maximum value of government expenditure was in 2014 at $3.0 billion.

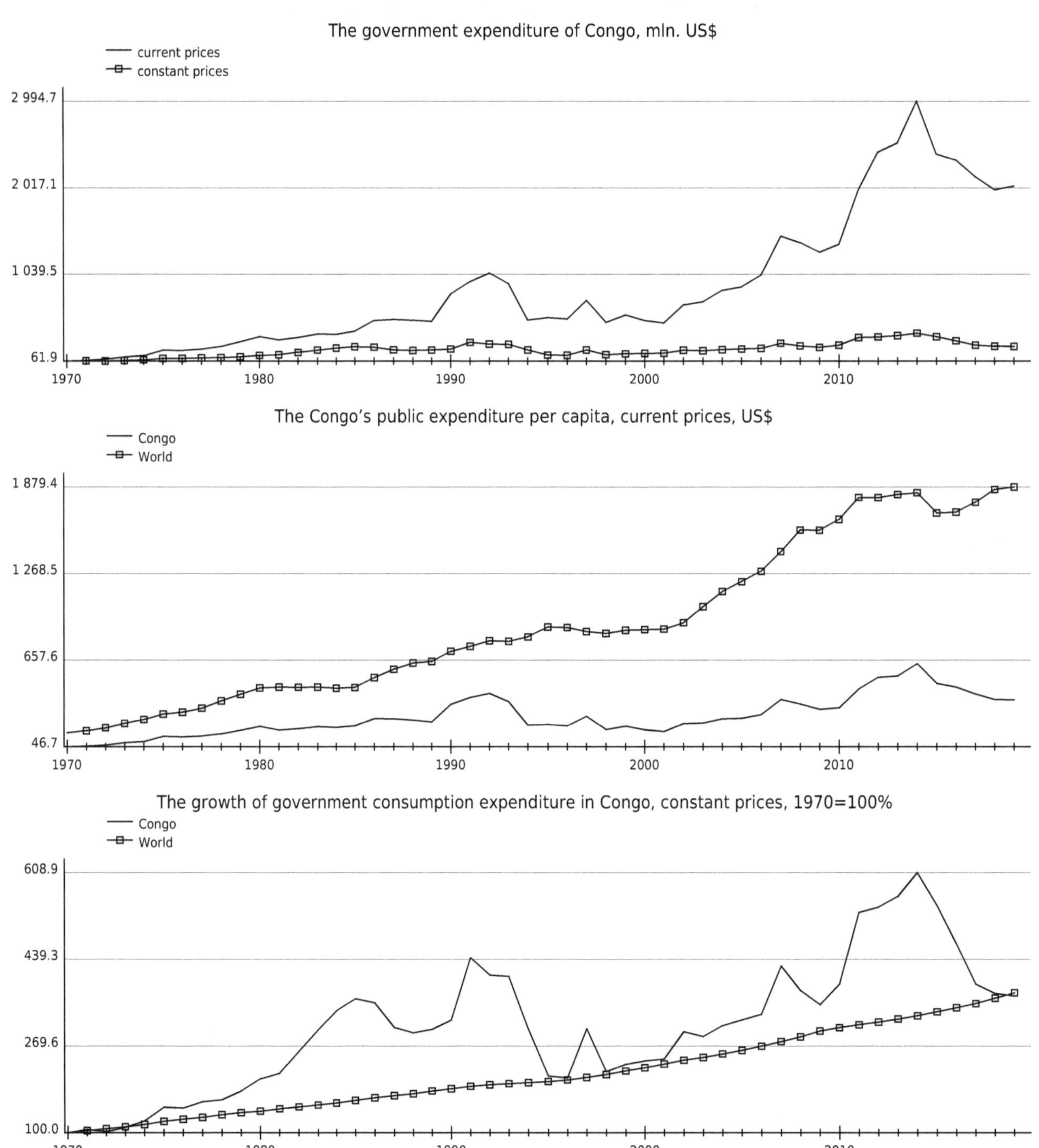

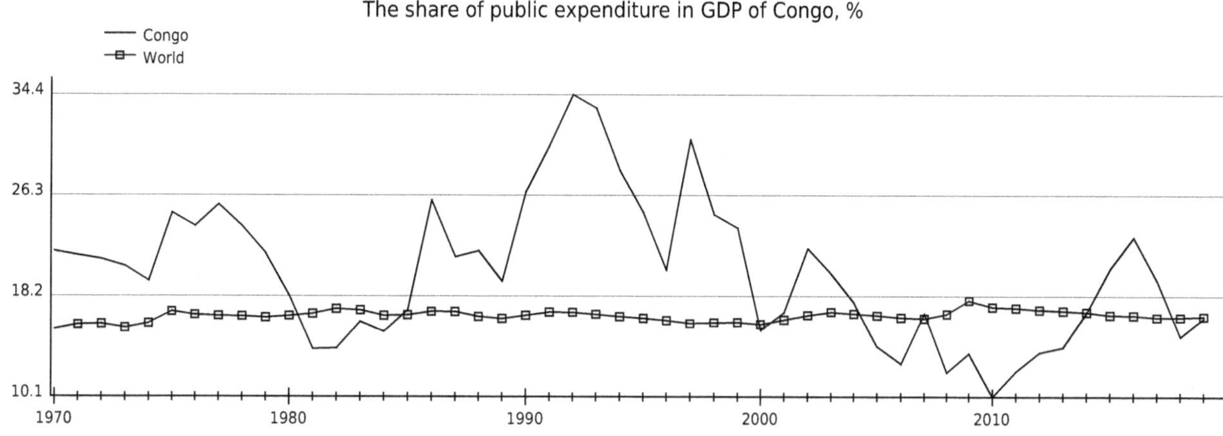

The 1970s

The Congo's government expenditure was $151.2 million per year in the 1970s, ranked 108th in the world, and was on a par with Bahrain ($154.9 million). The share in the world was 0.014%, and 0.48% in Africa.

The share of government expenditure in GDP of Congo was 22.7% in the 1970s, ranked 30th in the world.

The government expenditure per capita in Congo was $99.5 in the 1970s, ranked 116th in the world. The Congo's government expenditure per capita was less than government expenditure per capita in the world ($265.2) in 2.7 times, and was greater than public expenditure per capita in Africa ($77.1) by 29.2%.

The growth of government consumption expenditure in Congo was 6.8% in the 1970s, ranked 67th in the world, and was on a par with Ethiopia (6.7%), Greenland (6.8%), Western Africa (6.8%). The growth of government expenditure in Congo (6.8%) was greater than growth of government expenditure in the world (3.7%), was greater than growth of government consumption expenditure in Africa (4.9%).

Comparison with neighbors. The government expenditure of Congo was greater than in the CAR ($89.4 million); but less than in DR Congo ($2.0 billion), in Angola ($1.3 billion), in Cameroon ($385.8 million), and in Gabon ($351.2 million). The public expenditure per capita in Congo was greater than in DR Congo ($87.0), in Cameroon ($52.2), and in the Central African Republic ($45.7); but less than in Gabon ($544.9) and in Angola ($187.8). The growth of government consumption expenditure in Congo was greater than in Cameroon (5.7%), in Angola (0.84%), in the Central African Republic (-1.8%), and in DR Congo (-4.6%); but less than in Gabon (8.2%).

Comparison with leaders. The government consumption expenditure of Congo was less than in the United States ($285.9 billion), in the USSR ($117.3 billion), in Germany ($95.6 billion), in Japan ($78.0 billion), and in France ($64.5 billion). The government expenditure per capita in Congo was less than in the United States ($1 310.2), in Germany ($1 213.7), in France ($1 202.3), in Japan ($700.2), and in the USSR ($465.0). The growth of government expenditure in Congo was greater than in Japan (5.3%), in France (5.0%), in Germany (4.4%), and in the USA (0.94%); but less than in the USSR (7.2%).

The 1980s

The public expenditure of Congo was $417.7 million per year in the 1980s, ranked 107th in the world, and was on a par with Sri Lanka ($417.2 million), New Caledonia ($413.7 million), the Bahamas ($425.2 million). The share in the world was 0.017%, and 0.60% in Africa.

The share of government expenditure in GDP of Congo was 18.3% in the 1980s, ranked 77th in the world, and was on a par with Bhutan (18.3%), Italy (18.3%), San Marino (18.3%).

The government expenditure per capita in Congo was $205.8 in the 1980s, ranked 112th in the world, and was on a par with Nicaragua ($206.7), Northern Africa ($201.9), Eswatini ($211.0). The public expenditure per capita in Congo was less than government consumption expenditure per capita the world ($523.5) in 2.5 times, and was greater than government expenditure per capita in Africa ($128.3) by 60.4%.

The growth of public expenditure in Congo was 5.3% in the 1980s, ranked 46th in the world. The growth of public expenditure in Congo (5.3%) was greater than growth of government expenditure in the world (2.7%), was greater than growth of government consumption expenditure in Africa (1.8%).

Comparison with neighbors. The public expenditure of Congo was greater than in the CAR ($219.3 million); but less than in Angola ($2.7 billion), in DR Congo ($1.6 billion), in Cameroon ($1.1 billion), and in Gabon ($1.0 billion). The government expenditure per capita in Congo was greater than in Cameroon ($111.0), in the CAR ($88.0), and in DR Congo ($54.4); but less than in Gabon ($1 275.2) and in Angola ($271.6). The growth of public expenditure in Congo was greater than in Gabon (3.7%), in Cameroon (2.7%), in Angola (2.3%), in DR Congo (1.00%), and in the Central African Republic (-1.1%).

Comparison with leaders. The Congo's government consumption expenditure was less than in the United States ($665.3 billion), in Japan ($257.4 billion), in Germany ($203.7 billion), in the USSR ($181.1 billion), and in France ($159.8 billion). The government expenditure per capita in Congo was less than in France ($2.8 thousand), in the United States ($2.8 thousand), in Germany ($2.6 thousand), in Japan ($2.1 thousand), and in the USSR ($658.0). The growth of public expenditure in Congo was greater than in Japan (3.5%), in France (2.8%), in the USA (2.6%), and in Germany (0.98%); but less than in the USSR (5.4%).

The 1990s

The public expenditure of Congo was $720.0 million per year in the 1990s, ranked 118th in the world, and was on a par with Uganda ($737.9 million). The share in the world was 0.015%, and 0.81% in Africa.

The share of public expenditure in GDP of Congo was 28.0% in the 1990s, ranked 22nd in the world.

The government consumption expenditure per capita in Congo was $268.5 in the 1990s, ranked 118th in the world, and was on a par with Papua New Guinea ($267.4), Djibouti ($265.6), Samoa ($274.4). The government expenditure per capita in Congo was less than public expenditure per capita in the world ($824.8) in 3.1 times, and was greater than government consumption expenditure per capita in Africa ($126.1) in 2.1 times.

The growth of government expenditure in Congo was -2.5% in the 1990s, ranked 181st in the world, and was on a par with the Solomon Islands (-2.5%), Sierra Leone (-2.5%). The growth of government consumption expenditure in Congo (-2.5%) was less than growth of government consumption expenditure in the world (2.0%), was less than growth of government expenditure in Africa (1.6%).

Comparison with neighbors. The Congo's public expenditure was greater than in the CAR ($270.9 million); but less than in Angola ($4.4 billion), in DR Congo ($1.3 billion), in Cameroon ($1.1 billion), and in Gabon ($1.1 billion). The government consumption expenditure per capita in Congo was greater than in the CAR ($85.2), in Cameroon ($84.8), and in DR Congo ($33.1); but less than in Gabon ($996.6) and in Angola ($317.0). The growth of government consumption expenditure in Congo was greater than in DR Congo (-17.0%); but less than in Angola (3.5%), in Gabon (3.1%), in Cameroon (2.2%), and in the CAR (0.18%).

Comparison with leaders. The government consumption expenditure of Congo was less than in the United States ($1.1 trillion), in Japan ($651.8 billion), in Germany ($419.6 billion), in France ($325.4 billion), and in the UK ($234.6 billion). The Congo's public expenditure per capita was less than in France ($5.5 thousand), in Germany ($5.2 thousand), in Japan ($5.2 thousand), in the United States ($4.3 thousand), and in the United Kingdom ($4.1 thousand). The growth of public expenditure in Congo was less than in Japan (3.0%), in Germany (2.4%), in the United Kingdom (2.1%), in France (1.8%), and in the United States (1.3%).

The 2000s

The government consumption expenditure of Congo was $938.0 million per year in the 2000s, ranked 129th in the world, and was on a par with Mauritius ($942.1 million), Nicaragua ($932.5 million), Georgia ($951.7 million). The share in the world was 0.012%, and 0.63% in Africa.

The share of public expenditure in GDP of Congo was 15.1% in the 2000s, ranked 104th in the world, and was on a par with Vanuatu (15.0%), the CAR (15.1%), Asia (15.0%).

The government consumption expenditure per capita in Congo was $260.7 in the 2000s, ranked 142nd in the world, and was on a par with Bhutan ($264.3). The Congo's public expenditure per capita was less than public expenditure per capita in the world ($1 200.9) in 4.6 times, and was greater than government expenditure per capita in Africa ($164.8) by 58.2%.

The growth of government expenditure in Congo was 4.1% in the 2000s, ranked 91st in the world, and was on a par with Poland (4.1%), Morocco (4.1%). The growth of government expenditure in Congo (4.1%) was greater than growth of public expenditure in the world (3.1%), was less than growth of government consumption expenditure in Africa (5.0%).

Comparison with neighbors. The government expenditure of Congo was greater than in DR Congo ($922.3 million) and in the Central African Republic ($216.3 million); but less than in Angola ($7.1 billion), in Cameroon ($1.9 billion), and in Gabon ($1.3 billion). The Congo's government expenditure per capita was greater than in Cameroon ($109.8), in the Central African Republic ($54.1), and in DR Congo ($17.0); but less than in Gabon ($929.1) and in Angola ($371.3). The growth of government consumption expenditure in Congo was greater than in Gabon (3.8%), in Angola (-0.033%), and in the Central African Republic (-4.7%); but less than in DR Congo (7.7%) and in Cameroon (5.7%).

Comparison with leaders. The Congo's government expenditure was less than in the USA ($1.9 trillion), in Japan ($844.2 billion), in Germany ($520.1 billion), in France ($479.9 billion), and in the United Kingdom ($453.4 billion). The Congo's government consumption expenditure per capita was less than in France ($7.6 thousand), in the UK ($7.5 thousand), in Japan ($6.6 thousand), in the United States ($6.5 thousand), and in Germany ($6.4 thousand). The growth of government expenditure in Congo was greater than in the United Kingdom (2.9%), in the USA (2.2%), in Japan (1.7%), in France (1.7%), and in Germany (1.4%).

The 2010s

The Congo's public expenditure was $2.2 billion per year in the 2010s, ranked 126th in the world, and was on a par with Gabon ($2.2 billion), Georgia ($2.2 billion), Polynesia ($2.3 billion). The share in the world was 0.017%, and 0.68% in Africa.

The share of government expenditure in GDP of Congo was 15.6% in the 2010s, ranked 117th in the world, and was on a par with Asia (15.6%), Qatar (15.8%), Curaçao (15.8%).

The Congo's public expenditure per capita was $461.9 in the 2010s, ranked 150th in the world, and was on a par with Armenia ($464.7), South-Eastern Asia ($456.9). The Congo's public expenditure per capita was less than government expenditure per capita in the world ($1 785.1) in 3.9 times, and was greater than government consumption expenditure per capita in Africa ($281.0) by 64.3%.

The growth of public expenditure in Congo was 0.5% in the 2010s, ranked 170th in the world. The growth of government consumption expenditure in Congo (0.47%) was less than growth of government expenditure in the world (2.3%), was less than growth of public expenditure in Africa (3.0%).

Comparison with neighbors. The public expenditure of Congo was 0.29% higher than in Gabon ($2.2 billion) and 7.8 times higher than in the Central African Republic ($284.2 million); but 8.3 times lower than in Angola ($18.4 billion), 42.4% lower than in Cameroon ($3.9 billion), and 36.4% lower than in DR Congo ($3.5 billion). The government consumption expenditure per capita in Congo was 2.8 times higher than in Cameroon ($167.3), 7.3 times higher than in the CAR ($62.9), and 9.9 times higher than in DR Congo ($46.4); but 2.5 times lower than in Gabon ($1 161.8) and 30.8% lower than in Angola ($667.7). The growth of government consumption expenditure in Congo was greater than in the Central African Republic (0.14%); but less than in Cameroon (4.1%), in DR Congo (3.6%), in Gabon (1.8%), and in Angola (1.0%).

Comparison with leaders. The government consumption expenditure of Congo was 1 194.1 times lower than in the United States ($2.7 trillion), 755.7 times lower than in China ($1.7 trillion), 469.4 times lower than in Japan ($1.0 trillion), 324.7 times lower than in Germany ($721.6 billion), and 287.1 times lower than in France ($637.9 billion). The government expenditure per capita in Congo was 20.8 times lower than in France ($9.6 thousand), 19.1 times lower than in Germany ($8.8 thousand), 18.0 times lower than in the USA ($8.3 thousand), 17.7 times lower than in Japan ($8.2 thousand), and 2.6 times lower than in China ($1 197.3). The growth of public expenditure in Congo was greater than in the United States (0.0052%); but less than in China (8.3%), in Germany (1.9%), in Japan (1.3%), and in France (1.3%).

Chapter XIII. Household consumption expenditure

(including Non-profit institutions serving households)

The household expenditure of Congo increased from $543.7 million per year in the 1970s to $4.5 billion per year in the 2010s, that is by $4.0 billion or 8.3 times. The change occurred at $1.9 billion due to a 1.8-fold increase in prices, as also at $858.0 million due to a 1.5-fold increase in per capita rate, as well as at $1.2 billion due to the growing in population. The average annual growth in household expenditure is 3.5%. The minimum value of household consumption expenditure was in 1970 at $251.8 million. The maximum value of household consumption expenditure was in 2018 at $5.2 billion.

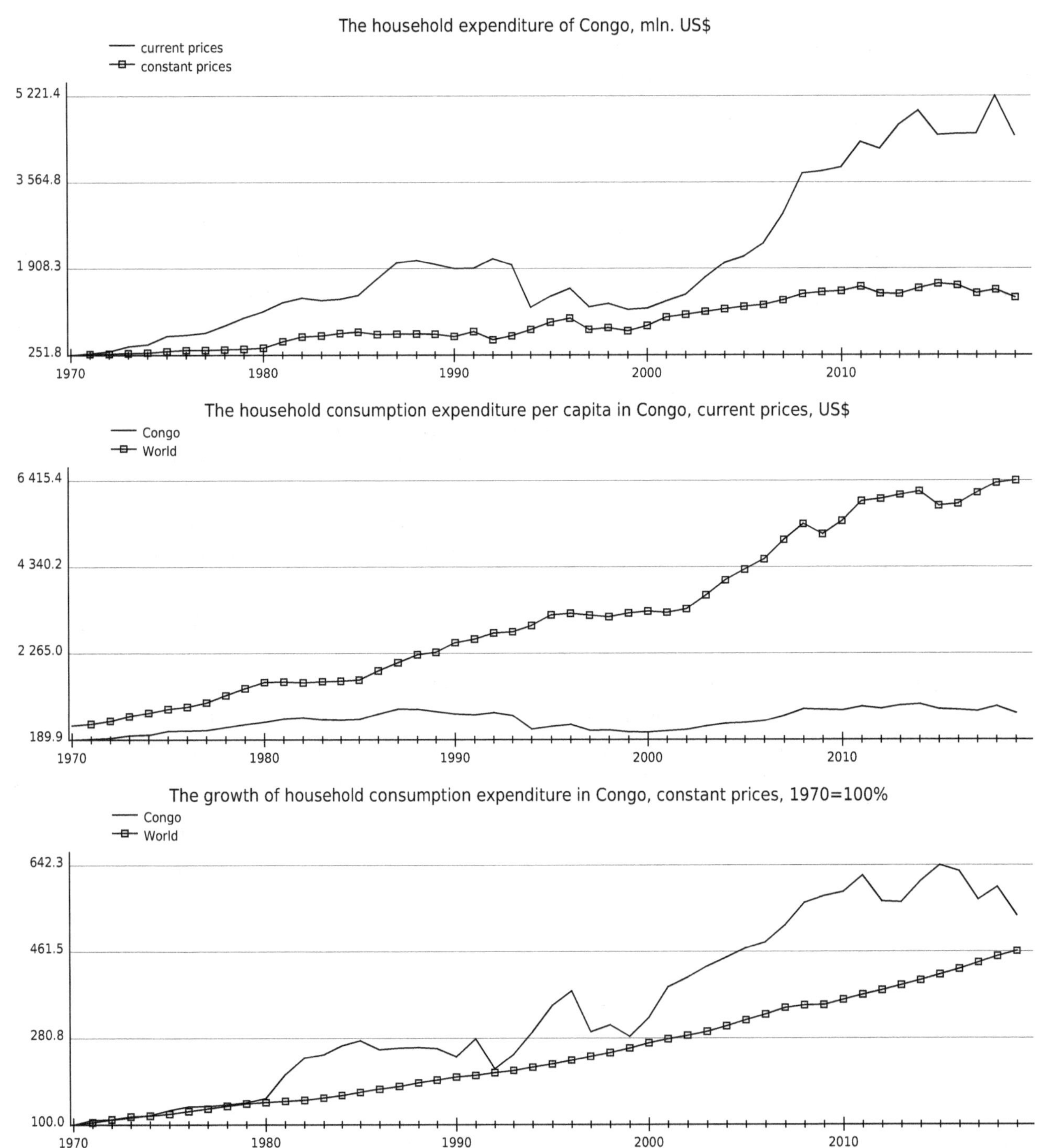

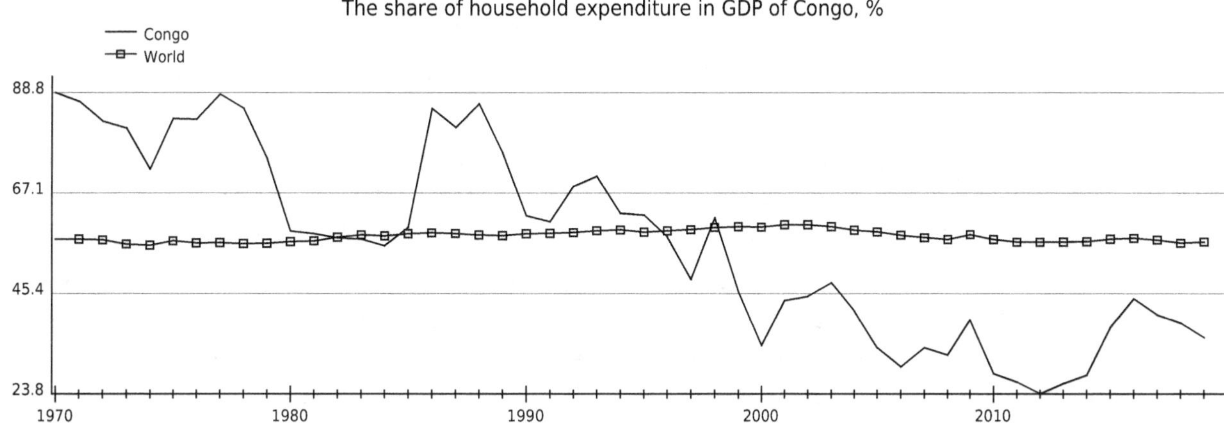

The 1970s

The Congo's household expenditure was $543.7 million per year in the 1970s, ranked 116th in the world, and was on a par with Qatar ($537.2 million). The share in the world was 0.015%, and 0.49% in Africa.

The share of household consumption expenditure in GDP of Congo was 81.6% in the 1970s, ranked 30th in the world, and was on a par with Saint Kitts and Nevis (81.5%), the Central African Republic (81.5%), Saint Lucia (81.7%).

The household consumption expenditure per capita in Congo was $357.9 in the 1970s, ranked 126th in the world, and was on a par with Eastern Asia ($359.2), Senegal ($360.0), Saint Vincent and the Grenadines ($360.4). The household expenditure per capita in Congo was less than household expenditure per capita in the world ($914.8) in 2.6 times, and was greater than household expenditure per capita in Africa ($271.0) by 32.1%.

The growth of household consumption expenditure in Congo was 4.3% in the 1970s, ranked 86th in the world, and was on a par with Portugal (4.3%), China (4.3%). The growth of household consumption expenditure in Congo (4.3%) was greater than growth of household consumption expenditure in the world (4.1%), was greater than growth of household consumption expenditure in Africa (4.1%).

Comparison with neighbors. The household expenditure of Congo was greater than in Gabon ($472.7 million) and in the Central African Republic ($454.8 million); but less than in DR Congo ($6.0 billion), in Cameroon ($2.5 billion), and in Angola ($2.1 billion). The household expenditure per capita in Congo was greater than in Cameroon ($343.1), in Angola ($304.0), in DR Congo ($263.3), and in the Central African Republic ($232.5); but less than in Gabon ($733.4). The growth of household consumption expenditure in Congo was greater than in the Central African Republic (3.2%), in Angola (-0.038%), and in DR Congo (-0.61%); but less than in Gabon (7.5%) and in Cameroon (6.6%).

Comparison with leaders. The household consumption expenditure of Congo was less than in the USA ($1.0 trillion), in the USSR ($310.6 billion), in Japan ($280.9 billion), in Germany ($277.8 billion), and in France ($180.7 billion). The household consumption expenditure per capita in Congo was less than in the United States ($4.7 thousand), in Germany ($3.5 thousand), in France ($3.4 thousand), in Japan ($2.5 thousand), and in the USSR ($1 231.6). The growth of household consumption expenditure in Congo was greater than in France (4.0%), in the USA (3.6%), and in Germany (3.6%); but less than in Japan (5.1%) and in the USSR (4.7%).

The 1980s

The household consumption expenditure of Congo was $1.5 billion per year in the 1980s, ranked 112th in the world. The share in the world was 0.018%, and 0.57% in Africa.

The share of household expenditure in GDP of Congo was 67.9% in the 1980s, ranked 75th in the world, and was on a par with Argentina (67.8%), Egypt (67.7%), Togo (68.3%).

The Congo's household consumption expenditure per capita was $763.3 in the 1980s, ranked 110th in the world, and was on a par with Peru ($769.5), Melanesia ($755.0), Guatemala ($748.0). The household expenditure per capita in Congo was less than household expenditure per capita in the world ($1 808.0) in 2.4 times, and was greater than household expenditure per capita in Africa ($497.8) by 53.3%.

The growth of household expenditure in Congo was 5.9% in the 1980s, ranked 26th in the world, and was on a par with Singapore

(5.9%). The growth of household consumption expenditure in Congo (5.9%) was greater than growth of household expenditure in the world (3.0%), was greater than growth of household expenditure in Africa (2.3%).

Comparison with neighbors. The Congo's household consumption expenditure was greater than in Gabon ($1.3 billion) and in the Central African Republic ($867.5 million); but less than in Cameroon ($7.2 billion), in DR Congo ($6.6 billion), and in Angola ($3.9 billion). The Congo's household consumption expenditure per capita was greater than in Cameroon ($720.1), in Angola ($398.8), in the CAR ($348.1), and in DR Congo ($223.8); but less than in Gabon ($1 616.4). The growth of household consumption expenditure in Congo was greater than in Angola (3.4%), in DR Congo (3.1%), in the CAR (3.0%), in Gabon (2.8%), and in Cameroon (1.8%).

Comparison with leaders. The Congo's household expenditure was less than in the United States ($2.6 trillion), in Japan ($945.6 billion), in Germany ($575.7 billion), in the USSR ($424.6 billion), and in the United Kingdom ($416.5 billion). The household expenditure per capita in Congo was less than in the USA ($10.9 thousand), in Japan ($7.8 thousand), in Germany ($7.4 thousand), in the United Kingdom ($7.4 thousand), and in the USSR ($1 542.8). The growth of household consumption expenditure in Congo was greater than in Japan (3.7%), in the UK (3.5%), in the United States (3.2%), in the USSR (3.0%), and in Germany (1.8%).

The 1990s

The Congo's household consumption expenditure was $1.6 billion per year in the 1990s, ranked 147th in the world, and was on a par with Turkmenistan ($1.6 billion). The share in the world was 0.0092%, and 0.41% in Africa.

The share of household expenditure in GDP of Congo was 60.4% in the 1990s, ranked 127th in the world, and was on a par with the Bahamas (60.5%), Northern Europe (60.5%), Hong Kong (60.4%).

The Congo's household consumption expenditure per capita was $578.6 in the 1990s, ranked 149th in the world, and was on a par with Cameroon ($566.9), Sri Lanka ($592.2). The Congo's household consumption expenditure per capita was less than household consumption expenditure per capita in the world ($2 963.9) in 5.1 times, and was greater than household consumption expenditure per capita in Africa ($532.7) by 8.6%.

The growth of household consumption expenditure in Congo was 0.9% in the 1990s, ranked 159th in the world, and was on a par with Djibouti (0.90%). The growth of household expenditure in Congo (0.90%) was less than growth of household consumption expenditure in the world (3.0%), was less than growth of household expenditure in Africa (2.6%).

Comparison with neighbors. The Congo's household expenditure was greater than in the Central African Republic ($869.9 million); but less than in DR Congo ($9.2 billion), in Cameroon ($7.6 billion), in Angola ($4.9 billion), and in Gabon ($2.1 billion). The household consumption expenditure per capita in Congo was greater than in Cameroon ($566.9), in Angola ($356.8), in the Central African Republic ($273.6), and in DR Congo ($226.5); but less than in Gabon ($1 921.2). The growth of household consumption expenditure in Congo was greater than in Cameroon (0.62%), in Gabon (-1.9%), in Angola (-2.1%), and in DR Congo (-3.8%); but less than in the CAR (1.4%).

Comparison with leaders. The Congo's household expenditure was less than in the USA ($4.9 trillion), in Japan ($2.3 trillion), in Germany ($1.2 trillion), in the UK ($884.5 billion), and in France ($783.0 billion). The household consumption expenditure per capita in Congo was less than in the USA ($18.5 thousand), in Japan ($18.2 thousand), in the United Kingdom ($15.3 thousand), in Germany ($15.2 thousand), and in France ($13.2 thousand). The growth of household consumption expenditure in Congo was less than in the United States (3.4%), in the United Kingdom (2.8%), in Germany (2.1%), in Japan (1.8%), and in France (1.8%).

The 2000s

The Congo's household expenditure was $2.3 billion per year in the 2000s, ranked 151st in the world, and was on a par with Kyrgyzstan ($2.3 billion), Monaco ($2.3 billion). The share in the world was 0.0083%, and 0.34% in Africa.

The share of household expenditure in GDP of Congo was 36.3% in the 2000s, ranked 196th in the world.

The household expenditure per capita in Congo was $628.5 in the 2000s, ranked 164th in the world, and eoas on a par with Yemen ($620.3), Ivory Coast ($636.7), Djibouti ($614.0). The household expenditure per capita in Congo was less than household expenditure per capita in the world ($4 208.2) in 6.7 times, and was less than household expenditure per capita in Africa ($735.9) by 14.6%.

The growth of household consumption expenditure in Congo was 7.4% in the 2000s, ranked 28th in the world, and was on a par with Saudi Arabia (7.4%). The growth of household consumption expenditure in Congo (7.4%) was greater than growth of household consumption expenditure in the world (3.0%), was greater than growth of household consumption expenditure in Africa (6.0%).

Comparison with neighbors. The Congo's household expenditure was greater than in the CAR ($1.2 billion); but less than in Angola ($13.7 billion), in Cameroon ($12.1 billion), in DR Congo ($10.8 billion), and in Gabon ($2.9 billion). The Congo's household consumption expenditure per capita was greater than in the Central African Republic ($291.4) and in DR Congo ($198.2); but less than in Gabon ($2.1 thousand), in Angola ($712.9), and in Cameroon ($690.3). The growth of household expenditure in Congo was greater than in Cameroon (3.7%), in Gabon (3.6%), in DR Congo (3.3%), and in the Central African Republic (3.3%); but less than in Angola (7.7%).

Comparison with leaders. The household expenditure of Congo was less than in the USA ($8.5 trillion), in Japan ($2.6 trillion), in Germany ($1.5 trillion), in the UK ($1.5 trillion), and in France ($1.1 trillion). The household expenditure per capita in Congo was less than in the United States ($28.8 thousand), in the UK ($25.0 thousand), in Japan ($20.4 thousand), in Germany ($18.9 thousand), and in France ($18.1 thousand). The growth of household expenditure in Congo was greater than in the USA (2.4%), in the UK (2.1%), in France (2.0%), in Japan (0.81%), and in Germany (0.46%).

The 2010s

The Congo's household expenditure was $4.5 billion per year in the 2010s, ranked 150th in the world. The share in the world was 0.010%, and 0.30% in Africa.

The share of household consumption expenditure in GDP of Congo was 31.7% in the 2010s, ranked 204th in the world.

The household consumption expenditure per capita in Congo was $938.4 in the 2010s, ranked 175th in the world, and was on a par with Mauritania ($955.1), Yemen ($916.5). The household expenditure per capita in Congo was less than household expenditure per capita in the world ($6 018.5) in 6.4 times, and was less than household expenditure per capita in Africa ($1 292.9) by 27.4%.

The growth of household consumption expenditure in Congo was -0.7% in the 2010s, ranked 199th in the world. The growth of household expenditure in Congo (-0.73%) was less than growth of household expenditure in the world (2.8%), was less than growth of household expenditure in Africa (3.3%).

Comparison with neighbors. The household expenditure of Congo was 2.6 times higher than in the CAR ($1.8 billion); but 11.6 times lower than in Angola ($52.3 billion), 5.8 times lower than in DR Congo ($26.2 billion), 5.1 times lower than in Cameroon ($22.9 billion), and 19.8% lower than in Gabon ($5.6 billion). The Congo's household consumption expenditure per capita was 2.4 times higher than in the CAR ($388.7) and 2.7 times higher than in DR Congo ($348.1); but 3.1 times lower than in Gabon ($3.0 thousand), 2.0 times lower than in Angola ($1 903.6), and 5.8% lower than in Cameroon ($996.2). The growth of household expenditure in Congo was greater than in the Central African Republic (-2.4%); but less than in DR Congo (5.5%), in Angola (5.1%), in Cameroon (4.5%), and in Gabon (4.3%).

Comparison with leaders. The Congo's household consumption expenditure was 2 700.5 times lower than in the United States ($12.2 trillion), 870.4 times lower than in China ($3.9 trillion), 661.7 times lower than in Japan ($3.0 trillion), 433.8 times lower than in Germany ($2.0 trillion), and 394.7 times lower than in the UK ($1.8 trillion). The household consumption expenditure per capita in Congo was 40.7 times lower than in the USA ($38.2 thousand), 28.9 times lower than in the United Kingdom ($27.2 thousand), 25.5 times lower than in Germany ($23.9 thousand), 24.9 times lower than in Japan ($23.4 thousand), and 3.0 times lower than in China ($2.8 thousand). The growth of household consumption expenditure in Congo was less than in China (8.3%), in the United States (2.4%), in the UK (1.8%), in Germany (1.4%), and in Japan (0.64%).

Chapter XIV. Food consumption

During the research period the food consumption grew in spices (in 5.3 times), sugar (in 2.9 times), meat (in 2.5 times), vegetables (in 2.4 times), milk (in 2.1 times), cereals (in 2.0 times), stimulants (by 84.6%), eggs (by 82.8%), alcoholic beverages (by 31.7%), fruits (by 28.9%), vegetable oils (by 12.6%), fish (by 1.6%), but fell in pulses (by 7.4%), starchy roots (by 39.1%).

These are the correlation coefficients between the GNI per capita in constant prices and the food consumption: meat (0.952), spices (0.944), cereals (0.892), sugar (0.859), eggs (0.822), fruits (0.788), stimulants (0.775), vegetables (0.687), milk (0.523), alcoholic beverages (0.38), vegetable oils (0.166), pulses (0.109), fish (-0.159), starchy roots (-0.781).

The 1970s

Kcal supply in Congo was 1 966.5 kcal/capita/day in the 1970s, ranked 127th in the world, and was on a par with Saudi Arabia (1 967.0 kcal/capita/day), El Salvador (1 962.9 kcal/capita/day), Laos (1 979.5 kcal/capita/day). Kcal supply in Congo was less than in the world (2 403.2 kcal/capita/day), and was less than in Africa (2 120.4 kcal/capita/day). Structure of kcal supply: starchy roots (54.1%), cereals (12.9%), vegetable oils (10.3%), fruits (4.8%), sugar (2.6%), and others (15.3%).

Protein supply in Congo was 35.9 g/capita/day in the 1970s, ranked 146th in the world, and was on a par with the Central African Republic (36.2 g/capita/day). Protein supply in Congo was less than in the world (65.0 g/capita/day), and was less than in Africa (54.9 g/capita/day). Structure of protein supply: starchy roots (20.3%), cereals (20.1%), fish (19.5%), meat (14.3%), pulses (6.2%), and others (19.6%).

Fat supply in Congo was 41.3 g/capita/day in the 1970s, ranked 108th in the world, and was on a par with Honduras (41.2 g/capita/day), Chad (41.1 g/capita/day), Eswatini (41.6 g/capita/day). Fat supply in Congo was less than in the world (55.1 g/capita/day), and was less than in Africa (43.8 g/capita/day). Structure of fat supply: vegetable oils (55.3%), meat (7.3%), fruits (3.5%), starchy roots (3.4%), fish (3.3%), and others (27.2%).

These are the levels of food consumption in the world rankings: 3rd - starchy roots (370.7 kg/capita/yr), 32nd - fish (23.5 kg/capita/yr), 52nd - vegetable oils (8.3 kg/capita/yr), 63rd - alcoholic beverages (28.2 kg/capita/yr), 86th - pulses (3.6 kg/capita/yr), 90th - fruits (48.4 kg/capita/yr), 111th - meat (11.7 kg/capita/yr), 127th - stimulants (0.20 kg/capita/yr), 132nd - vegetables (15.9 kg/capita/yr), 133rd - sugar (5.3 kg/capita/yr), 138th - milk (5.5 kg/capita/yr), 140th - spices (0.010 kg/capita/yr), 142nd - eggs (0.33 kg/capita/yr), 148th - cereals (31.5 kg/capita/yr).

The 1980s

Kcal supply in Congo was 2 111.6 kcal/capita/day in the 1980s, ranked 120th in the world, and was on a par with Zambia (2 112.7 kcal/capita/day), Yemen (2 109.3 kcal/capita/day), Botswana (2 108.9 kcal/capita/day). Kcal supply in Congo was less than in the world (2 572.3 kcal/capita/day), and was less than in Africa (2 241.9 kcal/capita/day). Structure of kcal supply: starchy roots (46.2%), cereals (17.2%), vegetable oils (11.3%), fruits (4.9%), sugar (4.1%), and others (16.3%).

Protein supply in Congo was 41.9 g/capita/day in the 1980s, ranked 144th in the world, and was on a par with Sierra Leone (42.1 g/capita/day). Protein supply in Congo was less than in the world (69.1 g/capita/day), and was less than in Africa (57.5 g/capita/day). Structure of protein supply: cereals (24.6%), fish (24.3%), starchy roots (15.2%), meat (13.6%), pulses (3.3%), and others (19%).

Fat supply in Congo was 47.1 g/capita/day in the 1980s, ranked 102nd in the world, and was on a par with Guinea (47.3 g/capita/day), Nigeria (47.6 g/capita/day). Fat supply in Congo was less than in the world (63.2 g/capita/day), and was greater than in Africa (46.6 g/capita/day). Structure of fat supply: vegetable oils (57.4%), meat (6.9%), fish (5.3%), cereals (3.7%), starchy roots (2.7%), and others (24%).

These are the levels of food consumption in the world rankings: 2nd - starchy roots (339.3 kg/capita/yr), 25th - fish (32.5 kg/capita/yr), 51st - alcoholic beverages (41.3 kg/capita/yr), 59th - vegetable oils (9.9 kg/capita/yr), 89th - fruits (52.7 kg/capita/yr), 114th - meat (13.3 kg/capita/yr), 118th - pulses (2.3 kg/capita/yr), 121st - sugar (8.9 kg/capita/yr), 126th - treenuts (0.010 kg/capita/yr), 130th - stimulants (0.22 kg/capita/yr), 132nd - milk (11.1 kg/capita/yr), 135th - vegetables (16.5 kg/capita/yr), 136th - spices (0.021 kg/capita/yr), 144th - eggs (0.37 kg/capita/yr), 146th - cereals (45.7 kg/capita/yr).

The 1990s

Kcal supply in Congo was 2 007.4 kcal/capita/day in the 1990s, ranked 151st in the world, and was on a par with Vietnam (2 010.9

kcal/capita/day), Laos (2 003.5 kcal/capita/day), Zambia (2 001.4 kcal/capita/day). Kcal supply in Congo was less than in the world (2 652.6 kcal/capita/day), and was less than in Africa (2 365.6 kcal/capita/day). Structure of kcal supply: starchy roots (41.5%), cereals (19.9%), vegetable oils (12.3%), fruits (5.4%), sugar (3.9%), and others (17%).

Protein supply in Congo was 43.2 g/capita/day in the 1990s, ranked 163rd in the world. Protein supply in Congo was less than in the world (72.1 g/capita/day), and was less than in Africa (60.1 g/capita/day). Structure of protein supply: cereals (25.1%), fish (18.7%), meat (17%), starchy roots (13.1%), vegetables (7%), and others (19.1%).

Fat supply in Congo was 47.9 g/capita/day in the 1990s, ranked 127th in the world, and was on a par with the Solomon Islands (48.1 g/capita/day), Bosnia and Herzegovina (48.1 g/capita/day), Burkina Faso (48.3 g/capita/day). Fat supply in Congo was less than in the world (69.0 g/capita/day), and was less than in Africa (48.6 g/capita/day). Structure of fat supply: vegetable oils (58.3%), meat (9.3%), fish (3.8%), cereals (3.3%), starchy roots (2.2%), and others (23.1%).

These are the levels of food consumption in the world rankings: 3rd - starchy roots (289.9 kg/capita/yr), 34th - fish (26.0 kg/capita/yr), 70th - vegetable oils (10.2 kg/capita/yr), 93rd - alcoholic beverages (22.8 kg/capita/yr), 95th - fruits (59.2 kg/capita/yr), 115th - pulses (2.7 kg/capita/yr), 116th - meat (18.5 kg/capita/yr), 124th - vegetables (33.7 kg/capita/yr), 143rd - sugar (7.9 kg/capita/yr), 153rd - milk (10.2 kg/capita/yr), 155th - treenuts (0.020 kg/capita/yr), 157th - stimulants (0.16 kg/capita/yr), 161st - spices (0.012 kg/capita/yr), 164th - eggs (0.43 kg/capita/yr), 167th - cereals (49.0 kg/capita/yr).

The 2000s

Kcal supply in Congo was 2 174.0 kcal/capita/day in the 2000s, ranked 151st in the world, and was on a par with Botswana (2 154.6 kcal/capita/day). Kcal supply in Congo was less than in the world (2 765.9 kcal/capita/day), and was less than in Africa (2 509.9 kcal/capita/day). Structure of kcal supply: starchy roots (36.7%), cereals (23.3%), vegetable oils (13.3%), sugar (6.6%), fruits (4.8%), and others (15.3%).

Protein supply in Congo was 44.8 g/capita/day in the 2000s, ranked 169th in the world, and was on a par with Angola (45.0 g/capita/day). Protein supply in Congo was less than in the world (76.5 g/capita/day), and was less than in Africa (65.1 g/capita/day). Structure of protein supply: cereals (29.4%), meat (16.5%), fish (14%), starchy roots (11.9%), vegetables (7.4%), and others (20.8%).

Fat supply in Congo was 51.3 g/capita/day in the 2000s, ranked 138th in the world, and was on a par with South-Eastern Asia (51.5 g/capita/day), Middle Africa (50.8 g/capita/day), Niger (51.7 g/capita/day). Fat supply in Congo was less than in the world (76.9 g/capita/day), and was less than in Africa (52.8 g/capita/day). Structure of fat supply: vegetable oils (63.9%), meat (8%), cereals (4.4%), milk (2.7%), fish (2.6%), and others (18.4%).

These are the levels of food consumption in the world rankings: 5th - starchy roots (277.1 kg/capita/yr), 60th - fish (21.1 kg/capita/yr), 72nd - vegetable oils (12.0 kg/capita/yr), 102nd - pulses (3.4 kg/capita/yr), 104th - alcoholic beverages (23.3 kg/capita/yr), 131st - meat (18.6 kg/capita/yr), 135th - sugar (14.5 kg/capita/yr), 153rd - milk (15.2 kg/capita/yr), 159th - stimulants (0.35 kg/capita/yr), 160th - treenuts (0.027 kg/capita/yr), 164th - eggs (0.59 kg/capita/yr), 166th - spices (0.016 kg/capita/yr), 171st - cereals (59.1 kg/capita/yr).

The 2010s

Kcal supply in Congo was 2 173.5 kcal/capita/day in the 2010s, ranked 160th in the world, and was on a par with Tanzania (2 174.3 kcal/capita/day), Zimbabwe (2 168.8 kcal/capita/day), Uganda (2 167.0 kcal/capita/day). Kcal supply in Congo was less than in the world (2 869.3 kcal/capita/day), and was less than in Africa (2 612.5 kcal/capita/day). Structure of kcal supply: starchy roots (35.2%), cereals (25%), vegetable oils (10.5%), sugar (6.8%), fruits (4.8%), and others (17.7%).

Protein supply in Congo was 50.6 g/capita/day in the 2010s, ranked 168th in the world, and was on a par with Zimbabwe (51.1 g/capita/day). Protein supply in Congo was less than in the world (80.6 g/capita/day), and was less than in Africa (69.0 g/capita/day). Structure of protein supply: cereals (27.3%), meat (22.9%), fish (14.3%), starchy roots (10.2%), vegetables (7.6%), and others (17.7%).

Fat supply in Congo was 46.3 g/capita/day in the 2010s, ranked 158th in the world, and was on a par with East Timor (46.7 g/capita/day). Fat supply in Congo was less than in the world (82.4 g/capita/day), and was less than in Africa (54.7 g/capita/day). Structure of fat supply: vegetable oils (55.5%), meat (12.6%), cereals (5.6%), fish (3.1%), starchy roots (2.1%), and others (21.1%).

These are the levels of food consumption in the world rankings: 6th - starchy roots (266.5 kg/capita/yr), 53rd - fish (23.8 kg/capita/yr), 83rd - alcoholic beverages (37.1 kg/capita/yr), 100th - vegetable oils (9.4 kg/capita/yr), 103rd - pulses (3.4 kg/capita/yr), 112th - fruits (62.4 kg/capita/yr), 116th - meat (29.2 kg/capita/yr), 137th - vegetables (37.7 kg/capita/yr), 138th - sugar (15.1 kg/capita/yr), 157th -

spices (0.053 kg/capita/yr), 158th - milk (11.5 kg/capita/yr), 164th - eggs (0.61 kg/capita/yr), 171st - cereals (64.5 kg/capita/yr).

Part V. Reproduction

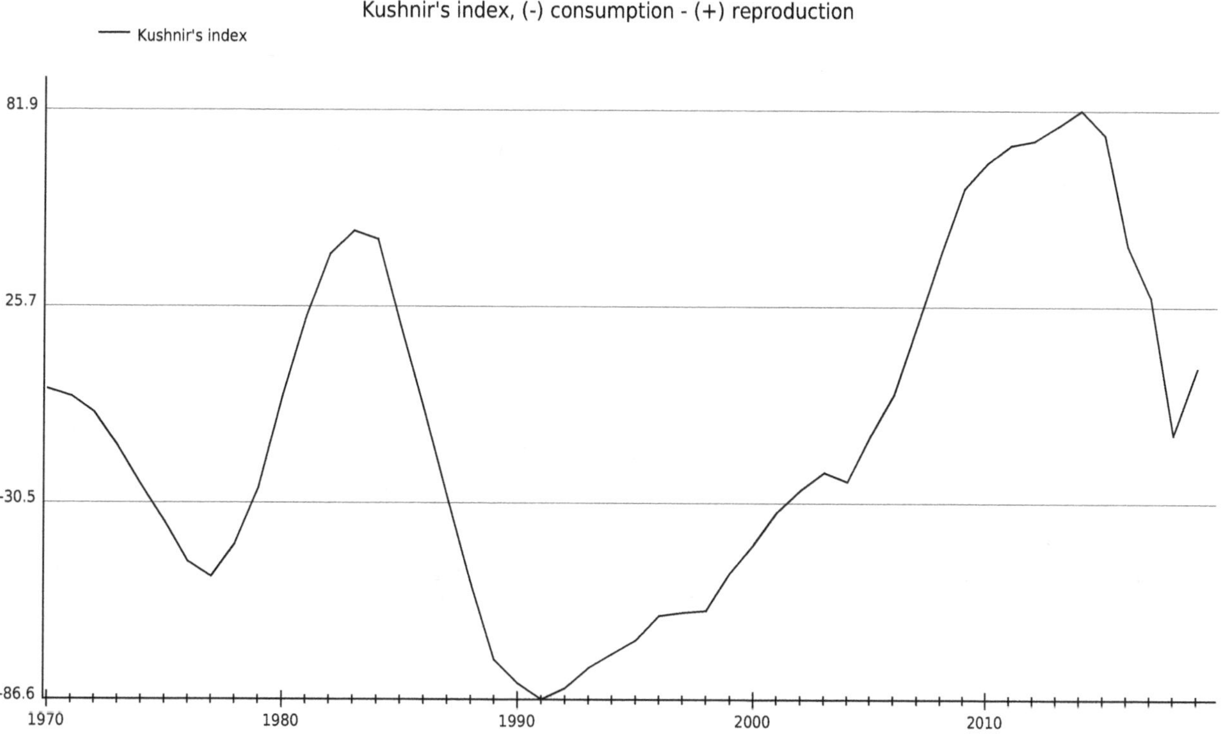

Chapter XV. Gross fixed capital formation

(including Acquisitions less disposals of valuables)

The gross fixed capital formation of Congo grew up from $322.2 million per year in the 1970s to $6.8 billion per year in the 2010s, that is by $6.4 billion or 21.0 times. The change occurred at $4.5 billion due to a 3.0-fold increase in prices, as also at $1.2 billion due to a 2.2-fold increase in per capita rate, as well as at $698.1 million due to the rise in population. The average annual growth in gross fixed capital formation is 3.2%. The minimum value of gross fixed capital formation was in 1970 at $145.6 million. The maximum value of gross fixed capital formation was in 2014 at $9.8 billion.

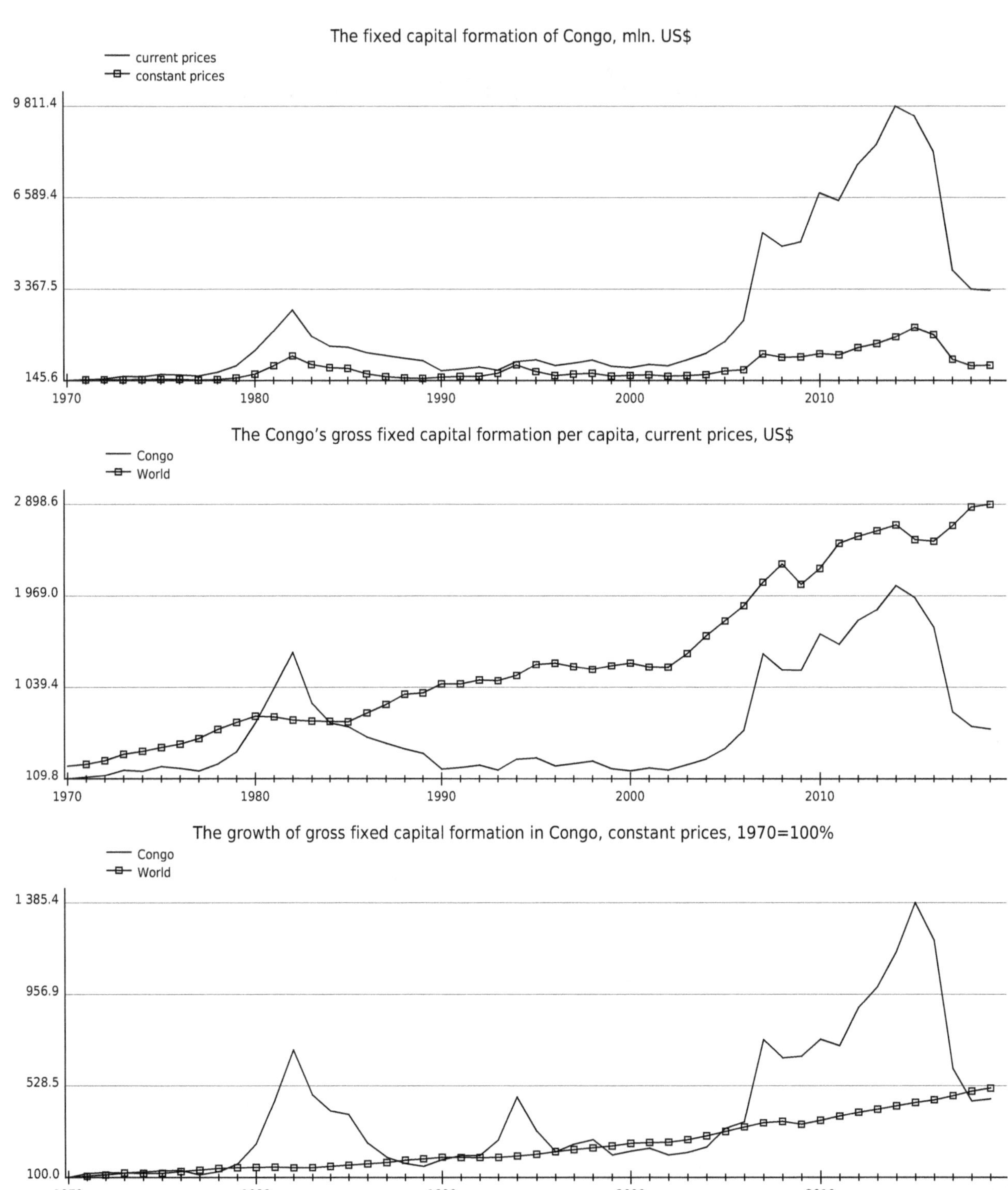

The fixed capital formation of Congo, mln. US$

The Congo's gross fixed capital formation per capita, current prices, US$

The growth of gross fixed capital formation in Congo, constant prices, 1970=100%

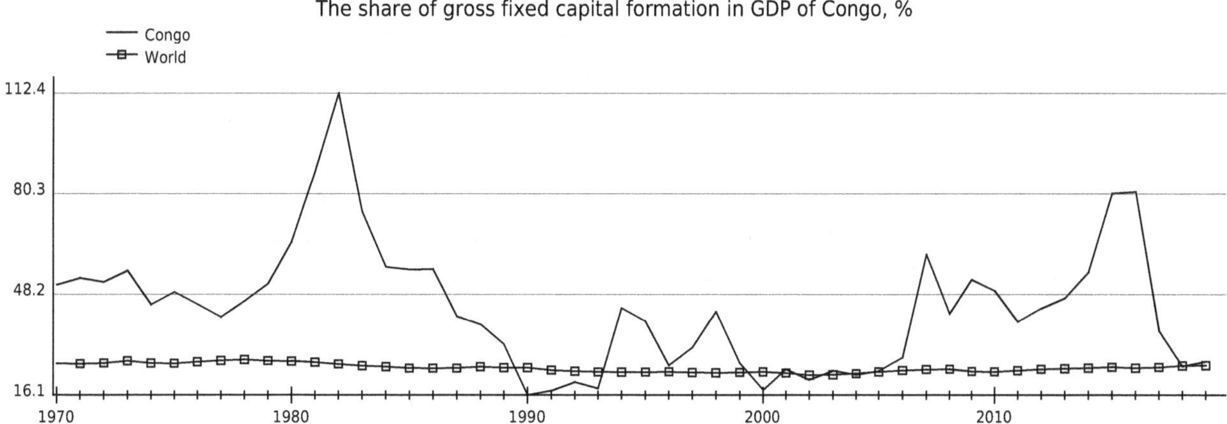

The 1970s

The gross fixed capital formation of Congo was $322.2 million per year in the 1970s, ranked 101st in the world, and was on a par with Zambia ($326.3 million). The share in the world was 0.018%, and 0.27% in Africa.

The share of gross fixed capital formation in GDP of Congo was 48.4% in the 1970s, ranked 5th in the world.

The Congo's fixed capital formation per capita was $212.1 in the 1970s, ranked 92nd in the world, and was on a par with Brazil ($212.9), the Federated States of Micronesia ($210.9). The Congo's fixed capital formation per capita was less than gross fixed capital formation per capita in the world ($433.5) in 2.0 times, and was less than fixed capital formation per capita in Africa ($289.8) by 26.8%.

The growth of gross fixed capital formation in Congo was 5.5% in the 1970s, ranked 93rd in the world, and was on a par with Tonga (5.5%). The growth of fixed capital formation in Congo (5.5%) was greater than growth of fixed capital formation in the world (4.2%), was less than growth of gross fixed capital formation in Africa (7.1%).

Comparison with neighbors. The Congo's gross fixed capital formation was greater than in the CAR ($74.9 million); but less than in DR Congo ($2.3 billion), in Angola ($1.1 billion), in Cameroon ($1.0 billion), and in Gabon ($833.3 million). The Congo's gross fixed capital formation per capita was greater than in Angola ($154.6), in Cameroon ($138.0), in DR Congo ($102.4), and in the Central African Republic ($38.3); but less than in Gabon ($1 293.0). The growth of fixed capital formation in Congo was greater than in DR Congo (4.8%), in Angola (0.22%), and in the CAR (-4.2%); but less than in Gabon (12.5%) and in Cameroon (6.9%).

Comparison with leaders. The Congo's gross fixed capital formation was less than in the USA ($381.9 billion), in the USSR ($214.6 billion), in Japan ($191.6 billion), in Germany ($125.8 billion), and in France ($82.9 billion). The Congo's gross fixed capital formation per capita was less than in the United States ($1 750.0), in Japan ($1 720.7), in Germany ($1 597.2), in France ($1 545.4), and in the USSR ($850.9). The growth of gross fixed capital formation in Congo was greater than in the United States (4.4%), in Japan (3.9%), in the USSR (3.2%), in France (2.7%), and in Germany (1.5%).

The 1980s

The gross fixed capital formation of Congo was $1.4 billion per year in the 1980s, ranked 77th in the world, and was on a par with Trinidad and Tobago ($1.4 billion). The share in the world was 0.037%, and 0.71% in Africa.

The share of fixed capital formation in GDP of Congo was 61.3% in the 1980s, ranked 3rd in the world.

The gross fixed capital formation per capita in Congo was $690.0 in the 1980s, ranked 70th in the world, and was on a par with Yugoslavia ($691.0), Romania ($674.1). The fixed capital formation per capita in Congo was less than fixed capital formation per capita in the world ($790.9) by 12.8%, and was greater than fixed capital formation per capita in Africa ($362.0) by 90.6%.

The growth of fixed capital formation in Congo was -0.7% in the 1980s, ranked 136th in the world, and was on a par with Western Asia (-0.73%). The growth of fixed capital formation in Congo (-0.73%) was less than growth of fixed capital formation in the world (2.5%), was greater than growth of gross fixed capital formation in Africa (-3.3%).

Comparison with neighbors. The Congo's gross fixed capital formation was greater than in Gabon ($1.3 billion) and in the CAR ($119.6 million); but less than in Cameroon ($3.3 billion), in DR Congo ($2.0 billion), and in Angola ($1.6 billion). The fixed capital formation per capita in Congo was greater than in Cameroon ($330.0), in Angola ($161.8), in DR Congo ($66.7), and in the Central African Republic ($48.0); but less than in Gabon ($1 575.5). The growth of gross fixed capital formation in Congo was greater than in Gabon (-2.9%) and in Angola (-6.4%); but less than in DR Congo (7.3%), in Cameroon (1.5%), and in the CAR (-0.33%).

Comparison with leaders. The gross fixed capital formation of Congo was less than in the United States ($958.4 billion), in Japan ($571.7 billion), in the USSR ($271.0 billion), in Germany ($238.1 billion), and in France ($164.3 billion). The gross fixed capital formation per capita in Congo was less than in Japan ($4.7 thousand), in the USA ($4.0 thousand), in Germany ($3.1 thousand), in France ($2.9 thousand), and in the USSR ($984.8). The growth of fixed capital formation in Congo was less than in Japan (4.8%), in the United States (3.1%), in France (2.4%), in the USSR (1.7%), and in Germany (1.4%).

The 1990s

The Congo's fixed capital formation was $679.5 million per year in the 1990s, ranked 128th in the world, and was on a par with Haiti ($672.5 million), Namibia ($669.3 million). The share in the world was 0.010%, and 0.55% in Africa.

The share of fixed capital formation in GDP of Congo was 26.5% in the 1990s, ranked 46th in the world, and was on a par with Suriname (26.4%), Cyprus (26.3%), Kosovo (26.6%).

The gross fixed capital formation per capita in Congo was $253.5 in the 1990s, ranked 133rd in the world, and was on a par with the Philippines ($253.0), El Salvador ($247.7). The fixed capital formation per capita in Congo was less than gross fixed capital formation per capita in the world ($1 183.8) in 4.7 times, and was greater than gross fixed capital formation per capita in Africa ($173.2) by 46.3%.

The growth of gross fixed capital formation in Congo was 3.1% in the 1990s, ranked 103rd in the world. The growth of fixed capital formation in Congo (3.1%) was greater than growth of fixed capital formation in the world (2.8%), was less than growth of fixed capital formation in Africa (3.2%).

Comparison with neighbors. The Congo's fixed capital formation was greater than in the Central African Republic ($145.6 million); but less than in Angola ($2.5 billion), in Cameroon ($2.1 billion), in Gabon ($1.1 billion), and in DR Congo ($883.1 million). The Congo's fixed capital formation per capita was greater than in Angola ($180.0), in Cameroon ($156.9), in the CAR ($45.8), and in DR Congo ($21.8); but less than in Gabon ($1 062.4). The growth of gross fixed capital formation in Congo was greater than in Gabon (1.9%), in Cameroon (1.5%), in the Central African Republic (0.38%), and in DR Congo (-14.3%); but less than in Angola (17.1%).

Comparison with leaders. The gross fixed capital formation of Congo was less than in the USA ($1.6 trillion), in Japan ($1.3 trillion), in Germany ($520.7 billion), in France ($299.3 billion), and in the UK ($250.0 billion). The gross fixed capital formation per capita in Congo was less than in Japan ($10.4 thousand), in Germany ($6.5 thousand), in the USA ($6.1 thousand), in France ($5.0 thousand), and in the UK ($4.3 thousand). The growth of gross fixed capital formation in Congo was greater than in Germany (2.4%), in the United Kingdom (1.7%), in France (1.5%), and in Japan (0.18%); but less than in the USA (4.8%).

The 2000s

The gross fixed capital formation of Congo was $2.3 billion per year in the 2000s, ranked 115th in the world. The share in the world was 0.021%, and 0.90% in Africa.

The share of gross fixed capital formation in GDP of Congo was 36.9% in the 2000s, ranked 12th in the world, and was on a par with Ghana (36.8%), Cape Verde (37.2%).

The Congo's gross fixed capital formation per capita was $637.7 in the 2000s, ranked 121st in the world, and was on a par with Armenia ($631.4). The Congo's fixed capital formation per capita was less than fixed capital formation per capita in the world ($1 690.7) in 2.7 times, and was greater than fixed capital formation per capita in Africa ($280.9) in 2.3 times.

The growth of fixed capital formation in Congo was 12.5% in the 2000s, ranked 20th in the world, and was on a par with Bahrain (12.4%), Montenegro (12.5%). The growth of gross fixed capital formation in Congo (12.5%) was greater than growth of gross fixed capital formation in the world (3.5%), was greater than growth of gross fixed capital formation in Africa (5.6%).

Comparison with neighbors. The Congo's gross fixed capital formation was greater than in Gabon ($2.2 billion), in DR Congo ($1.5 billion), and in the CAR ($160.2 million); but less than in Angola ($11.4 billion) and in Cameroon ($4.0 billion). The gross fixed capital formation per capita in Congo was greater than in Angola ($593.9), in Cameroon ($225.7), in the CAR ($40.1), and in DR Congo ($27.8); but less than in Gabon ($1 580.0). The growth of fixed capital formation in Congo was greater than in Cameroon (6.3%), in

Angola (2.8%), in Gabon (2.7%), and in the Central African Republic (-2.0%); but less than in DR Congo (14.1%).

Comparison with leaders. The gross fixed capital formation of Congo was less than in the USA ($2.8 trillion), in Japan ($1.2 trillion), in China ($1.0 trillion), in Germany ($557.7 billion), and in France ($463.9 billion). The gross fixed capital formation per capita in Congo was less than in the USA ($9.4 thousand), in Japan ($9.0 thousand), in France ($7.4 thousand), in Germany ($6.9 thousand), and in China ($782.2). The growth of gross fixed capital formation in Congo was greater than in France (1.6%), in the United States (0.43%), in Germany (-0.56%), and in Japan (-2.0%); but less than in China (13.4%).

The 2010s

The gross fixed capital formation of Congo was $6.8 billion per year in the 2010s, ranked 100th in the world. The share in the world was 0.035%, and 1.3% in Africa.

The share of gross fixed capital formation in GDP of Congo was 47.6% in the 2010s, ranked 3rd in the world.

The Congo's gross fixed capital formation per capita was $1 405.7 in the 2010s, ranked 111th in the world, and was on a par with Azerbaijan ($1 375.2). The Congo's fixed capital formation per capita was less than gross fixed capital formation per capita in the world ($2 621.1) by 46.4%, and was greater than gross fixed capital formation per capita in Africa ($440.4) in 3.2 times.

The growth of fixed capital formation in Congo was -3.5% in the 2010s, ranked 198th in the world, and was on a par with Iran (-3.5%). The growth of fixed capital formation in Congo (-3.5%) was less than growth of gross fixed capital formation in the world (4.1%), was less than growth of fixed capital formation in Africa (3.1%).

Comparison with neighbors. The Congo's fixed capital formation was 52.1% higher than in Gabon ($4.4 billion) and 18.1 times higher than in the CAR ($373.4 million); but 4.2 times lower than in Angola ($28.2 billion), 10.8% lower than in DR Congo ($7.6 billion), and 10.8% lower than in Cameroon ($7.6 billion). The gross fixed capital formation per capita in Congo was 36.8% higher than in Angola ($1 027.4), 4.3 times higher than in Cameroon ($329.1), 14.0 times higher than in DR Congo ($100.8), and 17.0 times higher than in the CAR ($82.6); but 39.7% lower than in Gabon ($2.3 thousand). The growth of gross fixed capital formation in Congo was less than in DR Congo (8.9%), in Cameroon (6.0%), in Gabon (4.9%), in the CAR (2.2%), and in Angola (-3.0%).

Comparison with leaders. The Congo's fixed capital formation was 668.7 times lower than in China ($4.5 trillion), 532.2 times lower than in the USA ($3.6 trillion), 178.9 times lower than in Japan ($1.2 trillion), 111.3 times lower than in Germany ($752.5 billion), and 103.0 times lower than in India ($696.8 billion). The gross fixed capital formation per capita in Congo was 2.6 times higher than in India ($535.2); but 8.0 times lower than in the USA ($11.3 thousand), 6.7 times lower than in Japan ($9.5 thousand), 6.5 times lower than in Germany ($9.2 thousand), and 2.3 times lower than in China ($3.2 thousand). The growth of fixed capital formation in Congo was less than in China (8.0%), in India (5.8%), in the United States (3.8%), in Germany (2.8%), and in Japan (1.8%).

www.ingramcontent.com/pod-product-compliance
Lightning Source LLC
LaVergne TN
LVHW062358180726
843498LV00009B/1350